Conservation of Wooden Objects

Conservation of Wooden Objects

A.S. Bisht

D.K.Printworld (P) Ltd.
New Delhi

&

National Museum Institute
New Delhi

Cataloging in Publication Data — DK
[Courtesy: D.K. Agencies (P) Ltd. <docinfo@dkagencies.com>]

Bisht, A. S., 1933-
Conservation of wooden objects/A.S. Bisht.
p. cm.
Includes bibliographical references (p.)
Includes index.
ISBN 13: 9788124604489
ISBN 10: 8124604487

1. Wood — Preservation — India. 2. Art objects — Conservation and restoration — India. I. Title.

DDC 709.54 22

ISBN 13: 978-81-246-0448-9
ISBN 10: 81-246-0448-7
First published in India in 2009

Publishers
D.K. Printworld (P) Ltd.
Regd. office : *'Sri Kunj'*, F-52, Bali Nagar
New Delhi - 110 015
Phones : (011) 2545 3975; 2546 6019; *Fax* : (011) 2546 5926
E-mail: dkprintworld@vsnl.net Web : www.dkprintworld.com

National Museum Institute
of History of Art, Conservation and Museology
C/o National Museum, Janpath
New Delhi - 110 011
Phones : (011) 2301 2106, 2301 1901, 2379 2249, 2379 2251
Fax : (011) 2301 1901, 2379 2249

Dedicated to

My Family

Preface

THE National Museum Institute (a deemed-to-be university) has been conducting its various courses in the three faculties including the faculty of Art Conservation for the award of MA degree since 1989. I am grateful to the authorities of the NMI, as it is more popularly known, for having associated me as a Visiting Faculty Member to teach one or two courses every semester, all these years while in service, and also after my retirement from the post of Chief Restorer and Head of Conservation at the National Museum, New Delhi. All these years I have contributed my bit in this endeavour so as to fulfil this commitment, with the result, our students are now successfully helping in the tasks in which they are involved including the ultimate task of Conservation of Cultural Property, as infrastructure facilities could be created to make available the personnel for various works in the various departments, governmental, private or otherwise.

As I look back at all the years from 1958 onwards, and as I grew older and older it has been my heartfelt desire to make available some textbooks for the future students of the NMI when some of us would not be able to continue to teach here for health reasons or otherwise. I have been an eyewitness to the upsurge in the care and conservation of cultural property in India and the growing needs for the same. There has been a general consciousness for the collective care and conservation by the various disciplines connected with the management of cultural property especially after the creation of the NMI. The students who pass out of this Institute have a better understanding of the various aspects of conservation management and its importance for the total safety of the collections while conducting the various activities in a museum starting from acquisition, conservation, study, storage, display, exhibitions, transportation and handling of the artefacts. NMI, therefore, has grown into a grand banyan tree under which many students take shelter. Needless to say, older people are gradually being suitably replaced after their retirement by our students and they are doing very well. Truly, *guru*s (teachers) might remain as *guṛ* (lump of molasses) but the *celā*s (students) may become *śakkara* (sugar). I think it is a matter of great satisfaction for the teachers for all times to come.

Initially, I was allotted courses to teach aspects of conservation for all faculties — Technical Study and Documentation, Deterioration of Organic and Inorganic objects and also Conservation of Organic objects made of wood, textiles, bone, ivory, leather and ethnographic artefacts. During these years I have already published two books, through a private publisher *Conservation Science and Scientific Aspects of Heritage Study* which covered the topics I have been teaching. Now I am very happy to say that God-willing, it is within my reach to prepare books specifically on various topics as stated above, and the NMI has agreed to help. Thanks to the NMI to have agreed to see my dream come true. Fortunately all the VCs of the NMI have been very kind to me since I was associated with them in one way or the other from the very beginning while serving the National Museum and wherever they were earlier. I would fail in my duty if the names of these VCs are not mentioned. They are: the late Dr L.P. Sihare, the late Dr R.C. Sharma, Dr S.S. Biswas, Dr R.D. Choudhury, and Dr A.K.V.S. Reddy.

I have used the slides and photographs of the artefacts as photo credits belong to the National Museum, many of which I had taken myself while I was Head of the Laboratory and are being used now. I duly acknowledge this fact. I thank the then Head of the Wood Anatomy Branch, Forest Research Institute, Dehra Dun Dr S.K. Purkayasth and other officers including my brother-in-law, Shri B.S. Negi, one of the Sr. Research officers of that branch who helped me while I was attending their three month's training course on wood anatomy in the mid-1960s. It was a great help in initiating the work of identification of woods used in making statues and other architectural structures in the past. I also take this opportunity to thank the present VC of the NMI for his continued support and confidence and for keeping me active in the profession even at this age. I would also like to thank all other colleagues at present and in the past at the NMI for their support. I am also very thankful to my family members for their continued support even though I might have ignored their personal expectations from me all these years. God bless them all. I am also grateful to the publishers for their help.

Contents

List of Illustrations

Plates

Figures

1

Introduction

WOODEN Art objects, conservation techniques of which are going to be dealt with in this book are composed of organic materials. These have their origin from mother nature in the form of plants and have been made suitable for our daily use or artistic creativity. We must, therefore, have an appropriate understanding of their origin and the relation to the various sets of organisms such as animals, plants, trees and humans which were all having life at one time and have passed from the juvenile to adult stages and finally to death since death (felling down of trees) is the end. It has, therefore, played an important role in the development of what we see around us today as part of the ecology (*Pls.* 1 & 2).

On earth, nothing can live entirely on its own. Of all living beings plants in nature are the only ones to make their own food by a process called photosynthesis in the presence of sunlight and conduct sap from the soil made by the micro-organisms like fungi and bacteria which break down the dead plants and animals into minerals which get absorbed by the soil and help in the growth of the plants in the form of sap as food besides absorbing the carbon dioxide released by us humans and also animals. All of these natural living things, therefore, are connected to each other in an invisible and complicated way. Plants collect energy from the Sun, and animals feed on plants. When plants and animals die, their remains do not pile up, instead, fungi and bacteria break them down, so that they can be recycled and re-used. In nature, living things always look after themselves. Flowering plants provide insects with sugary nectar and in return, insects help plants by spreading pollen from flower to flower, in a partnership called symbiosis. Forests are the home to many different animals, but they are also valuable in other ways. The roots of trees help to bind the soil together and stop it being washed away when it rains heavily and starts to flood (*Pls.* 3 & 4) as seen in the photos.

Their leaves take in carbon dioxide and give off oxygen, keeping the atmosphere fit to breathe by living beings. The chlorophyll in their leaves withdraws carbon dioxide from the air, converts it into sugar and starches, and give off free oxygen as a byproduct. In the growth process of the tree these simple carbohydrates are then converted into cellulose, hemicellulose and lignin. In mountains, forests also act as living crash barriers against avalanches. This co-operative attitude in between them, has a very subtle relationship with nature to keep the ecological balance.

History of Use of Wood

Most of the remains of wood indicate to us the history of the past, the way of life of our ancestors, their creations and the message of the civilization of each period. For their personal and household use they met all their requirements of items which were easily available not very far from their habitat. Plant materials, therefore, were most suited because of their easy availability, ease in handling and their resilience. So, man, in earlier times, used wood to build shelters to reside in and also protect them from the extremities of the climate, to make household implements for help in their day-to-day work, to make statues for artistic and religious needs, to meet their daily needs of fuel to keep them warm, to make artefacts, ritual objects, for architectural purposes and to cook food. Wood was then available in abundance in nature. However, we also find many examples of painted wood carvings, wood panels and statues after the seventeenth century CE (*Pls.* 5 & 6).

Examples of different woods having been used for different purposes, other than paintings, during the Indus Valley Civilization are reported from the excavation accounts of sites at Haṛappā and Mohenjo-dāṛo in the Indian subcontinent and for making large buildings and structures. The earliest example of wood as an archaeological evidence comes from a coffin made of wood datable to 2000 BCE. The top plank of this coffin was reportedly made of *devadāra* (*Cedrus deodara*) and rose wood (*Dalbergia latifolia*) was reportedly used to make the side planks. Both of these two woods have an aroma which keeps the insects away and it seems that our ancestors had the knowledge of their properties. The wood used for making a mortar for pounding grains was *Zizyphus spp*. This reveals that the Harappans were not only aware of the shock absorbing quality of this timber but also of the fact that this is one of the few woods that seasons well in the form of logs and was therefore suitable for the purpose.

Although the wood remains from Hastināpur do not clearly indicate whether these were used for firewood or charcoal yet there is little doubt that the people of this civilization had some idea of the woods that had high calorific value. *Śīśama* and *kurchī* the two types of wood recovered from this excavation are considered, even today, good for fuel. People living nearabout the dawn of the early historic period in the fourth century BCE, during the reign of Candragupta Maurya, knew about the properties of different types of wood that would prove useful in the construction of palaces in Pāṭaliputra, the modern Patna. The species of wood has been identified by the author as belonging to the *sāl* tree (*Shorea robusta*) which is again a very strong and durable wood. Similarly the wood used at Śiśupālgaṛh for the construction of a wooden gate in Orissa proves that the people of that period also knew about the strength and durability of *Acacia sp. Babūla* or *kīkara*. The wooden statue from the Sun God temple, Katarmal (Almora, Uttarakhand) belonging to the sixteenth century CE was identified as *devadāra* (*Cedrus deodara*) and the gateway from the same site was built of *śīśama* (*Dalbergia sissoo*). These are to this day preserved in the collection of the National Museum, New Delhi.

From the species of wood chosen by the people of those days, it is clear that they knew the basic properties of these woods very well before using them. Similarly the wood used to make houses and other structures in the areas prone to earthquakes in the Himalayan region and some from Gujarat, especially the doorway, in the collection of the National Museum, New Delhi were identified by the author as *sāl* (*Shorea robusta*) (*Pls*. 7 & 8). The use of this particular wood shows their concern about safety because the wooden facades are made of this very strong and durable wood.

We have a recording also on wood, now surviving, which has been reported from the caitya cave at Bhaja in western India where two wooden ribs on the entrance gate have an inscription in Brāhmī script engraved on them. This inscription says that this caitya was earlier made of wood and has now been transferred in stone. As reported by M.N. Deshpande, Ex. Director General of Archaeological Survey of India, this inscription is datable to the second century BCE. Wooden panels, showing parts of temple architecture with or without designs, door frames and lintels are very popular in Gujarat, West Bengal, Andhra Pradesh, J&K, and Rajasthan and reveal the taste of our people which also includes the folk element in them. Decorated and lacquered furniture like bedposts, low stands, centre tables, often inlaid with rich ivory, silver and even gold, were largely manufactured during the sixteenth to eighteenth centuries CE and continue even today in India (*Pls.* 9 & 10).

It is not definitely known when man first began to use wood. Some authorities are of the opinion that this practice started during the Old Stone Age, when man was on the look-out for a digging tool in his search for food. The Stone Age hunters, early types of modern humans, had slowly spread across the face of earth reportedly from Africa. Actual evidence of the use of wood by man has been recorded for the first time from the excavations of the sites of the New Stone Age. In the Indian subcontinent no site of the Stone Age has so far produced any evidence of the use of wood. Our earliest records go back only to the proto-historic period, i.e. from 3000 BCE to the historic era. The first evidence, in this regard, comes from the Indus Valley Civilization. People, at that point in time, started making tools and weapons to cut wood from the thick forests. They lived in caves or shelters or huts, wore leaves/barks of trees to cover their bodies and to protect them from the unfavorable climate. They also knew how to make fire by rubbing dry sticks or two pieces of stone together some 5000 years ago. The first farmers of Middle East recognized the wild seeds and started farming (*Pls.* 11 & 12) after clearing the forests.

India is one of the half-a-dozen countries of the world where the prehistoric art is very rich and alive. The other areas which are known for this art are France, Spain and Italy in Europe, the northern and southern parts of Africa and Australia. In these caves, early man decorated the roofs and walls with many scenes showing the early life of these people and their interests. This is true of all of these sites irrespective of their geographical locations in India or elsewhere. This proves that early humans were alike the world over. With experience they also knew how to store their farm produce in pots of wood and woven baskets made of fibrous plant materials. Wooden tablets from Central Asia (*Pl.* 13), as an ancient writing material, and wooden architectural objects (with a *pūrṇaghaṭa*) belonging to the third century CE (*Pl.* 14) are in the collection of the National Museum, New Delhi. Under this category of objects we find wooden objects in various forms such as covers for the ancient manuscripts on papyrus, palm leaf, birch bark and *sāñcīpaṭa*. The central Asian collections are very important from the art historian's point of view. Chinese and Turkish artefacts in wood belonging to a wide span of centuries preserved with the efforts of Sir Aurel Stein and other members of his team (1913-16) are kept in England, Germany and India.

This study would not only help in knowing these artefacts better but also clarify the circumstances of those days and the difficulties our ancestors faced during their lifetime. The development of science and technology introduced new tools which made their jobs, of fulfilling their day-to-day needs of basic nature like building shelters to sustain their life easier. At a time in the evolution of civilization, of growing population and of industrialization, much of this heritage faced considerable danger. The question of priorities and means to carry out programmes to study, interpret and safeguard them has acquired prime importance for the national and international community as well as the relevant organizations.

In an article in *The Hindustan Times* dated 25 May 2006 Nayanjot Lahiri, a Professor of History at Delhi University, emphasized the need for an in-house facility for dating our past archaeological remains, and has reported that the nineteen fifties of the last century gave us the radio carbon dating method as one of the most important developments. The Bose Institute of Sciences, Kolkata was the first to do the radio carbon dating of wood from the ancient site of Pāṭaliputra. Subsequently, a radio carbon laboratory was set up, first at the Tata Institute of Fundamental Research in Mumbai, and then at the Physical Research Laboratory, Ahmedabad. The PRL at Ahmedabad no longer does carbon dating. More recently an AMS (Accelerator Mass Spectrometry) dating laboratory was set up in Bhubaneswar. While surfing the Internet I was amazed to find that an American Professor of Chemistry, City University of New York, Brooklyn, N.Y. had reported that when a wooden piece from a riverside doorway was subjected to the carbon dating test, it proved that the Taj existed centuries before Shah Jahan's times. Later the DGA was requested to allow him one more visit so that the findings could be confirmed. The DGA suggested that there was no need for such a study since the Taj Mahal is well dated on documentary evidence; moreover the BARC and PRL in India are also seized of the problem and the issue may be treated as closed. I had also advocated a Dating Laboratory for ASI in my book *Scientific Aspects of Heritage Study* (2004) on the basis of my long experience as I felt the urgent need for such a facility to set at rest such issues in the field of scientific study of our heritage of artistic, historic, archival and archaeological significance.

Man in his selfish interests and casual attitudes, greed, apathy and mismanagement has forgotten the subtle interdependence between him and Nature by polluting it to a point of no return. This has not only affected the environment but also the heritage which was created by his ancestors. Instances are plenty where man himself has invited his own doom as would be seen from the extinction of many species around him of plant/animal origin, resulting in the disappearance of his own valuable creations due to his apathy. Most of the wooden objects are very delicate and fragile, prone to decay, have been in use over the centuries, have seen many varied tropical and sub-tropical climatic conditions, have been in different geographical locations and have been passed on from one generation to another making their care dependent on many people during their lifetime before entering into a collection with the governmental bodies or otherwise. In many cases as a consequence of their continuous use they have suffered unintentionally. Do we realize why we do not find all the artefacts of the past made of organic materials like wood, birch bark, palm leaf, etc. still surviving today? Only those artefacts have managed to survive which had some sort of maintenance by way of preservation techniques indigenous or otherwise available. This proves that preservation can provide the necessary longevity to plant materials.

Literary Evidences

Our ancient texts such as the Vedas, the Upaniṣads, the Purāṇas, etc. which were, for example, on palm leaves, birch bark and other allied materials, have either perished with time or have been lost to posterity due to various reasons including ignorance. Similarly wooden puppets from south India and the South Asian countries especially Indonesia, where I had an opportunity to be in the year 1971 to start the Bronze Conservation Project at the Directorate of Museums, Jakarta under a JRD 3rd grant, remind us of our ancient contacts with that beautiful island country since the tenth century CE because these puppets have been preserved at Jogjakarta, Prambanan, Borobudur and Bali. During this assignment when I was in Bali I was convinced that more than 90 per cent of the population was Hindu and it was difficult to decide if I was in south India or Bali. There were a large number of temples in Indonesia with carvings made of wood (*Pl.* 15).

Wooden structures (*Pl.* 16), which I had an opportunity to see in Japan in the year 1982 during the International Seminar on Conservation of Wooden Cultural Property, have a perfect similarity with our traditional wooden temples and monastery structures from the northern parts of India, especially from Ladakh, Sikkim and parts of Himachal Pradesh besides some of the adjoining countries of Nepal or Bhutan, where such structures are still present in the earthquake prone areas where wood was abundantly available in the form of dense forests. Australian aboriginal

Bark painting has its problems as is seen in the picture (*Pl.* 17). The main problem being warping and flaking.

Governmental concern at the 1992 Rio Earth Summit has forcefully emphasized the sustainable, environment-friendly, global ecology. The efforts of governments alone cannot achieve these goals without the support of people at large. Let us learn to live with nature rather than abuse it. An equilibrium has to be established between human needs and the God-gifted ecology around us. Rarely is an environmental issue more important or complex than global warming has been. Burning of coal, oil and natural gas to heat our homes, to power our cars, and illuminate our cities producing carbon dioxide and other greenhouse gases as by products is the main danger here. Similarly, deforestation and land clearing also release significant quantities of harmful gases which cause all living beings as well as the artefacts around us to decay. Let us not aggravate the damage to our heritage to the extent that it crosses the limits and the damage caused is beyond repair. All the concerned experts should pool their resources together to save not only the art objects but also the environment around us so that the achievement of our ancestors can be saved for posterity.

All literature shows that many substances of animal and vegetable origin were known from ancient times, which were termed as organic. The use of herbs as medicine has been known to Indians from very early times. More than a century ago all substances then known were classified on the basis of sources from which they were derived. It was assumed that the organic compounds could be produced only by living matters present in nature. It had become evident, however, that most of the compounds formed by living cells (plants and animals) contained carbon. Hence, the emphasis was shifted from the origin to composition, and organic compounds came to be considered as those containing carbon and hence objects of wood also contained carbon.

In 1828, the German chemist Friedrich Wohler heated ammonium cyanate and obtained the organic compound urea. The urea formed in this way was identical to the urea isolated from urine. This was the beginning of the era when scientists could synthesize an organic compound from inorganic material. Hence organic materials/objects were defined to contain carbon, with a few exceptions. These exceptions included carbon monoxide, carbon dioxide, carbon disulphide, carbonates, bicarbonates, cyanides, thio-cynides, cyanates, and carbides which are dealt with in inorganic chemistry and are studied due to their properties and not for their composition.

Composition is the basis for organic matter/objects. Today there are over three million known organic compounds, and several thousand new compounds are synthesized each year. Carbon has the ability to bond successively with other carbon atoms to form chains of varying lengths and shapes. This property of carbon is called catenation and is responsible for the variety and large number of organic compounds. A large number of artefacts made from plant products in our collections today, besides the ones which were being used earlier and are still in vogue in some areas such as palm leaf and barks of trees like birch bark and in north-east India bark of *sāñcīpaṭa,* wood used for shelters and furniture, objects of daily use like puppets made of wood, decorative art works made of wood with inlay of ivory and bone, statues for worship, are all made of organic matter. It is also observed that organic chemistry and organic objects have influenced the lives of our people and sometimes even changed the course of our civilization. Since most of these objects are made from living matter they decay faster than their inorganic counterparts. What our ancestors have created over the centuries and the millennia reflects the historic development upon which we build and from which we draw inspiration in order to build our future. The manifold products of the arts and crafts, the rich testimonies of social and religious life, the wealth of written documents, the articles of daily use, were seldom made with longevity in mind or that they would last over great periods of time. They were repaired when they were worn out or replaced when they were no longer of use. We in India laboured under a tropical climate, with rapid fluctuations of humidity and temperature that foster the activity of animal and vegetable parasites and hardly allow organic materials such as wood to survive unprotected for any length of time without being subject to damage. Catastrophes such as floods, storms, fires and earthquakes also caused untold losses. A thorough and conscientious consideration of the areas of damage, often involving a meticulous investigation of the causes of the damage, is thus the basic prerequisite for the development of suitable methods of restoration and conservation that are capable not only of repairing the existing damage, but also of assuring the object of lasting protection from further decay. My attempts, therefore, in the following chapters would be to highlight and discuss almost every detail of the methods used, based on my long experience to ensure the total health of the objects. In this book I will describe the information about the conservation and restoration of the following wooden objects.

1. Wood carvings, and
2. Polychrome wooden statues/structures which are plant products.

I expect to cover most of the objects which normally come under this classification. The collections belong to the various Museums in India which I happened to scan while I was the Head of Conservation, National Museum, New Delhi. The information which had been collected at that time is being utilized now in the wider interests of Cultural Heritage Management. A large amount of information is based on my notes and long association with the National Museum from 1958 to 1991 as well as the National Museum Institute (a Deemed University), with which I have been associated as a Visiting Faculty Member, in the Department of Conservation, since its very inception. To many readers it would serve as a basic information; yet to some it may appear stale. But I wish to stress the fact that I have been regularly teaching at the National Museum Institute for the last 20 years and also that I have been updating the relevant information thus making it a latest view on the subjects which I have been teaching to the satisfaction of the authorities as well as my students.

Location of Wooden Artefacts

Most of the museums that house important collections of wooden objects are either under the direct control of, or are indirectly financed by, the Government of India, institutions of national importance, the State museums spread throughout the country, the local body museums and the individual trust museums, private collections of big business houses and the elite. I visited all these, plus the collections abroad during my tenure in the National Museum, New Delhi. The wooden artefacts we find here are either in the form of statues (big and small) painted or carved, or architectural remains like temples and chariots (rathas) (*Pls.* 18 & 19), painted or carved household items, inlay work and lacquered works for decorative purposes. Some of them have been recovered from excavations done at historical sites.

These objects have to be studied in greater and wider detail in order to better understand them from the point of view of their origin, source material, composition, structure, properties, their method of making, and the environmental parameters responsible for their decay. This study should be undertaken to determine the mechanism of alteration and deterioration due to physical, mechanical, chemical, biological, man-made and inherent factors, to diagnose the decay, examine the methods of treatment and recording the preventive and curative techniques adopted for their conservation. Only after this stage are the objects made ready for an entry into a collection, after giving them the proper treatment, handling them with care, and after transporting them, storing or displaying them under proper conditions. The documentation and examination of the health of the objects at periodic intervals should be taken up as a regular programme for all the collections wherever they exist — it is the ultimate responsibility of every one working for an institution.

Accountability should be the rider to fix the responsibility for any lapse as a deterrent to apathy, ignorance and carelessness. There should be an in-house conservation unit in every institution so that artefacts could be kept in good condition and where help in conservation could be provided immediately if any decay was noticed or reported by the curators of the collections. All curators have to ensure that there is no damage to the artefacts while in storage, on display, or while handling or during transportation. There should be a regular interaction between the conservation staff and curators. Needless to mention that the specialized storage facilities, proper gallery management, scientific handling using adequate techniques and mechanized transportation have to be provided as per modern scientific and technological advances as is the practice the world over. Conservation is an integral part of almost all the activities in a museum. They support the museum's efforts to exhibit and interpret the collections for the here and now and preserve them for the enjoyment and education of future generations. The basic principles which underline a museum's conservation work are:

1. Prevention;
2. Reversibility; and
3. Aesthetic responsibility.

Most restorations are designed to be invisible to the naked eye. The experts take measures to make the objects look complete while not obscuring the visible differences between the original works and their restorations.

The objects made of organic materials are comparatively more prone to decay, and, therefore, not many examples of this category would survive the forces which promote decay. Today the world has already lost many of its architectural and archaeological cultural heritage and unless urgent measures are taken for conserving them, there is no saying if the moveable or immoveable heritage would be in the same state of preservation as it is today. While the need for proportionate infrastructural facilities would need to be strengthened in future for the conservation of our cultural heritage, we can at least document them using modern gadgets that use digitalization techniques. This would at least record the continuous change, the previous problems and past interventions. These records could then be used to identify an emergency so that urgent steps to rectify the damage could be taken in time. As a matter of fact, these days the importance of documentation extends beyond its use as a tool for conservation and a record for posterity.

In the various chapters of this book, while dealing with the details of conservation of organic plant products, I hope to cover a particular category of objects beginning with its source, material, structure, composition, method of making, factors of deterioration, various parameters of the agencies that cause decay and the alterations which ensue as a result. I would then proceed to enumerate and explain the conservation techniques used to restore their lost glory. And last but not the least I would describe the after-treatment care, namely preventive conservation technology which has to be ensured for its total safety/longevity over the years to come. I also intend to cover the shortcomings of these techniques, and the prospects of improving these techniques based on research to explore what would be the best for this category of artefacts.

This would help in better understanding them, the mechanism of their decay, diagnosis of the problem, chalking out the best available conservation strategy to determine the best remedial measures of combating the decay, and to identify a scientific process of restoration that does not in any way affect its artistic and historic value and overall aesthetics. Art historians usually are not in favour of intervention with the present state of an object but they need to understand the effect of the decaying process which hampers its originality. When the artist made an artefact I am sure this was not the way it looked then. Conservation attempts to remove the harmful accumulations which may be inflicting some form of invisible decay, that hides the beauty of the artefact. An expert conservator tries to retrieve an artefact's original look without altering its basic features as far as possible. He does not have to introduce his own art to it by reconstructing it. The difference between restoration and reconstruction has to be understood by one and all. A conservator on the other hand has to ensure that after the treatment the artefact should in no case look new. The so-called old look should be maintained at all costs.

Need to Review Our Policy of Acquisition

Some of the art dealers of disrepute want to earn easy money by employing artists to reconstruct the damaged objects or changing a new object into an old one as an art of deception (*Pls.* 20 & 21) and bringing an unwanted and not bargained for dishonour to the experts of the Art Purchase Committee where artefacts are acquired for collection on a simple visual examination and by basically relying on the memory of the members of the Art Acquisition Committee.

With due regards to them and their authority, I am tempted to say that such a situation could be easily avoided if the artefacts being offered are thoroughly examined first in a laboratory. Based on the reports of the laboratory the acquisitions may then be either selected or rejected. This cannot be insisted on at present because of the prevailing system and it would take time to change the rules. The museums in India need to restrain at least temporarily the activity of art acquisition to some extent, for the time being, and firmly deter the entry of fakes in their collections, even though they may be a good work of art and craft.

2

Wood as Material for Art Objects

Source of Wood

WE have a very rich flora consisting of dense tropical forests that are spread through the length and breadth of the country. West Bengal, Gujarat, Kerala, Tamil Nadu, Himalayan region, Uttar Pradesh, Assam, etc. have yielded many wooden objects and architectural pieces. There is literary evidence to show that wood was extensively used for making statues, carvings and in architecture in ancient India. An Indian ship made of wood is represented in the murals at Ajantā (*fig.* 1). Likewise a canoe in wood and a ceremonial ship is depicted on the stone gateway of *stūpa* 1 at Sāñcī (*fig.* 2). This only proves its use in India from very early periods. But most unfortunately the wood remains of ancient Indian wood carvings of the period earlier than seventh-eighth centuries CE are not many.

A large variety of timbers were used by our artisans in the past. Some of the surviving timber samples which have been identified by the researchers including me are:

1. Teak (*Tectona grandis*);
2. *Śīśama* (*Dalbergia sisso*);
3. Rose wood (*Dalbergia latifolia*);
4. *Devadāra* (*Cedrus deodara*);

5. Sandal wood (*Santalum album*);
6. Himalayan Ash (*Fraxinus floribunda*);
7. *Sāl* (*Shorea robusta*);
8. *Mahuā* (*Madhuca latifolia*);
9. *Babūla* (*Acacia sp.*);
10. *Kaṭahala* (*Artocarpus sp.*);
11. *Bera* (*Ficus spp.*); and
12. *Salai* (*Boswellia serrata*) to mention a few.

Most of these species come from two sources "hardwoods," and "softwoods" or coniferous or cone bearing trees having needle-like leaves among gymnosperms (*Pl.* 22), which are usually grown on hills and consist of three types of cells namely:

1. Trachieds;
2. Wood rays; and
3. Parenchyma.

The trachieds are about 3-5 mm in length and 0.02–0.04 mm in diameter. They conduct sap from the soil and also provide body to the wood. The wood rays take food from sunlight through the process of photosynthesis and the parenchyma stores the food needed for the growth of the tree when alive.

"Hardwoods" or angiosperms (*Pl.* 23) which have broad leaves and usually grow on planes or at average altitudes, consist of four types of cells. Samples of these types of wood have been taken from a tenth century wooden statue of Sun God from Katarmal, Almora (*fig.* 3) and a wooden doorway (*fig.* 4) from the same temple in the collection of the National Museum, New Delhi.

Hardwoods mainly consist of:

1. (i) Vessels or pores; (ii) Fibre; (iii) Wood rays; and (iv) Parenchyma.
2. Sap transportation is carried out by vessels or pores directly from the soil. These vessels or pores are elongated and constructed from individual cells joined end to end over a considerable distance. Bordered pits occur in these vessel walls. Fibres provide mechanical strength through their long narrow cells having closed pointed ends. Wood rays are used for making food from sunlight and storage of food is achieved through the parenchyma cells. It is interesting to note that almost all of the woods identified for making artefacts in the past in India are hardwoods except *devadāra* which is a soft, aromatic wood. This aroma is a deterrent for insects which thus makes it durable. Thus there is a need to identify a large number of woods to come to some conclusion regarding this statement.

Successful conservation of wooden artefacts is dependent upon a knowledge of wood structure and types. Softwoods, or gymnosperms, have needle-like leaves that prevent snow to accumulate because of the conical shape of the leaves. Gymnosperms are considered non-porous because they lack vessels/pores. It is critical that conservators know the category of wooden species that they are treating. In many instances, it is equally important that a wooden object is identified according to the species level in order to successfully conserve the wood.

Field Identification of Wood

Identification of common Indian timbers is an important

study under wood anatomy. Though people who work on them or work in the forest department can recognize timbers from their vast experience this type of identification does not always prove true. Each timber or group of very closely related timbers possesses a characteristic structure, especially on the cross-section which is due to an arrangement of wood cells that produces a distinctive pattern. Hence the identification of timbers depends in part on these varying anatomical structures and in part on some physical properties like colour, odour, texture, grain and heaviness, etc. This identification offers a fascinating study which tests the powers of observation, and proficiency is attained only after much concentration and perseverance.

Softwoods are non-porous, i.e. they do not possess pores whereas hardwoods are porous having pores or vessels. I shall now discuss these two types of woods and describe their main anatomical features individually. This method is called field identification which is a basic as well as a very essential step in the field of wood identification. It is customary in wood identification to study wood in three planes namely the transverse or cross-section, the tangential section, i.e. at right angles to the rays, and the radial section, i.e. parallel to the rays. The last two are longitudinal planes. It is interesting that the same wood appears differently on these three surfaces. For microscopic or field identification we need only a sharp knife and a pocket lens with a magnifying power of about 10 to 12 times. First of all one must find out the end surface or transverse section in a wood specimen. This is done by making a preliminary cut at right angles to the wood fibres and thus locating the direction of rays on the end surface. These rays look as parallel lines on the end surface. Thus we make a small area of the end surface by making one clean cut. The method of making the cut is very important; it must be made in one action and not as small series of jabs; the knife blade should be very nearly parallel to the end surface so as to ensure that the prepared surface is very nearly transverse and not oblique. The cut should always be made along the rays from the bark towards the centre of the tree. With a little experience this becomes easy and one gets used to it.

After the end surface has been prepared, the subsequent procedure depends on several circumstances. In every case the first point to decide is whether pores are present or not; this settles as to which of the two main classes of timber (hardwoods and softwoods) the sample belongs. Having now decided whether the sample is porous or non-porous we proceed with the further observations. The following general properties are noted first in a proforma as described below:

1. Whether the heart wood and sap wood are distinct or indistinct.
2. The colour of the heart wood or sap wood.
3. Estimated hardness as seen from the resistance offered by the wood when cut by a sharp knife across the grain.
4. The presence or absence of lustre.
5. Odour to be noted if present.
6. Grain to be noted whether straight or interlocked.
7. Texture to be noted whether fine or coarse or medium.
8. Fluorescence, if any.

Next step is to note the gross structure with the pocket lens. For non-porous timbers the following are to be noted:

1. Visibility of growth rings on cross and longitudinal sections.
2. Transition from early to late wood whether gradual or abrupt.
3. Resin canal present or absent:
   (i) if present, their distribution, i.e. whether scattered or in a row, and
   (ii) size and visibility on cross and longitudinal section.
4. visibility of rays.

For porous woods the first step is to note whether wood is ring porous or diffuse porous. Ring porous timbers are those in which the pores are found in the beginning of the growing season, i.e. early or spring wood are much larger than in the ring or late wood or summer wood. Diffuse porous woods are those in which the pores exhibit little or no variation in size in one seasonal growth. Ring porous woods are very few in India such as teak, mulberry, tūna, etc. Most of the porous woods in India are diffuse porous. In these cases the following observations are made:

(i) Whether ring porous or diffuse porous

(ii) Growth rings — whether distinct or indistinct and how delimited

(iii) Pores or vessels:

  (a) visibility to naked eye whether visible without lens or with lens

  (b) distribution and arrangement and shape,

whether solitary or in radial multiples or in radial chains or oblique groups

(c) inclusions — whether tylosses or gummy deposits present or not and their colour

(d) visibility on tangential surface

(iv) Parenchyma — whether

(a) vessicentric — *babūla*

(b) aliform — *koko*

(c) aliform to aliform confluent — *śīśama*

(d) initial or terminal — *laural* and *teak*

(e) banded — *poon*

(f) diffuse in aggregate — *haldu*

(g) reticulate — *ebony*

(h) no parenchyma — *salai.*

(v) Rays, (a) size and visibility in cross and radial surface, (b) arrangement

(vi) ripple marks to be mentioned only when present — *kañju* and *bījasāl.*

(vii) Gum canals to be mentioned only when present with reference to size and distribution — *gurjan* and *sāl.*

(viii) Pith flakes to be mentioned only if present — *śīśama.*

(ix) Ray flakes to be mentioned only if present — *śemala.*

Having noted all these in a wood sample we now take the help of a Dichotomon's Key and identify the specimen. Some people follow a punch card key system in which every timber has been allotted one card and its properties have been noted in it by notching the present characters of a particular timber. By a process of elimination, all other cards are individually separated on the basis of observations till at last only one card remains; thus the identification is complete. FRI, Dehradun has prepared such a key that can be had from them.

The above identification can also be confirmed under a microscope at low magnification < than 40 ×. Thin sections 15μ are prepared, stained and mounted and the photomicrographs can be compared with the published data. For staining the cellulose and lignin, separate solutions of 3 per cent Hematoxiline in water and 1 per cent Safranin in alcohol are repetitively used. A thin slice from a completely saturated wood sample is cut by using a microtome and it is mounted permanently with DPX mounting at 25° C.

Material of Wood

Wood is mostly composed of three complex molecules cellulose, hemicellulose and lignin. These three components together form the cell wall, the fundamental unit of the tree. Cellulose is a complex organic polymeric material containing:

1. carbon, hydrogen and oxygen and has a tendency to convert back into primary glucose molecules;
2. it has originated from plant world and is a natural product having directional properties;
3. it belongs to the polar hydroxyl group which makes it hygroscopic and, therefore, has a natural affinity for moisture to be absorbed; and

4. it undergoes hydrolysis resulting in a shorter chain monomer that has a lower molecular weight that helps to convert the polysaccharide into monosaccharide and ultimately into various sugars. Chemically it consists of about 40 to 60 per cent cellulose, 15 to 25 per cent hemicellulose and 15 to 40 per cent lignin. Besides, woods also have some colouring matters, waxes and resins which contribute to its appearance and other features which are estimated as 1 per cent of the total contents. I have seen the internal structure of various timbers after my brief training in the science of Wood Anatomy at the great institute at FRI, Dehradun, who have been pioneer in this field (Chaudhury and Ghosh) and have helped the Indian Archaeological Survey of India and some museums of the country to know their possessions better. To me it has been a God-given chance to peep into His creations, the inside of plants and trees.

Properties of Wood

Woods have a cellular structure and the actual wood substance is in the cell walls and the walls of the vessels and tracheids. The basic cellulose component of a cell wall at the molecular level is known as microfibril. The cell wall which is largely composed of cellulosic microfibrils is constructed from two or three distinct layers — the outside or primary wall, the secondary wall and an innermost tertiary wall. When the tree is alive the moisture content of green wood may be several times its dry weight and exists in three ways in the wood tissue. Wood being cellulose is also a food for biodetergins.

Water in Wood

There is considerable amount:

1. of free water in cell cavities and in the pores/vessels;
2. of bound water in the cell walls; and
3. of the protoplasts of parenchyma cells of the sap wood.

All of them contain free water, bound water and water of the protoplasts respectively. However, when the tree is cut it loses the free water of the vessels and parenchyma first and gradually comes in equilibrium with the RH (relative humidity) of the environment and becomes related to the bound water of the cell walls. Later it gradually responds with it and loses its moisture content when dry conditions occur or gains it when the conditions become more humid. When the cell walls and other cellular substance in wood are saturated with water it is termed as the fibre saturation point. Moisture content in wood is directly proportional to RH of the surroundings and at this stage the wood is said to be seasoned. It is customary to express the moisture content of wood in terms of its oven dry weight and its percentage can be calculated by the formula as given under.

$$\text{Moisture percentage} = \frac{\text{wt. of green wood} - \text{wt. of oven dry wood}}{\text{wt. of oven dry wood}} \times 100$$

When wood absorbs and holds moisture (bound water) it is called as hygroscopic. It can hold about 30 per cent water of the weight of green wood. The ability of wood to take up and hold moisture is due to the fact that the ultra-microscopic particles of cell wall substance are surrounded by films of water which reach their ultimate diameter at about 30 per cent moisture content. This is called its fibre saturation point at which no shrinkage occurs. Living protoplasts are found in both longitudinal and ray parenchyma as long as it is a part of the sap wood and water enters into the composition of protoplasm to the extent of 90 per cent of its weight. This does not hold good for heart wood since the living protoplasts have now entirely disappeared and all moisture above the fibre saturation point must be considered as free moisture. Once the wood gains equilibrium with its new environment, all the free water whether in the vessels or in the parenchyma disappears and only the bound water in the cell walls remains which reacts with the RH.

Table 1

RH (%)	*Moisture Content (%) (based on oven dry weight)*
100	30.0
90	21.5
70	13.5
50	9.5
30	6.5
10	3.25
0	0.0

PHYSICAL STRUCTURE

The wood of the outer cone of a tree trunk is known as the sap wood and the inner part of the cone is called heart wood. Sap wood is usually different in colour, lighter in tone, less dense than the heart wood of the log. The sap wood portion has a higher water content than the heart wood portion as the cells are coarse in nature and are thus porous. The heart wood portion is generally more dense and compact. This makes it more resistant to weathering, less prone to wood destroying insects and fungi as the biodetergins often shun them since they prefer to eat and thrive on the less dense part of the sap wood which has more moisture than the heart wood. The growth of a tree in length (primary growth) is traceable to the apices of twigs and roots. Growth in thickness results from a lateral meristem (cambium) which underlies the bark and which through cell division provides for increase in thickness.

As pointed out earlier, trees grow in two ways, in length and in thickness. While the cambium through cell division forms wood centripetally and phloem centrifugally, there is no reason to infer that like amounts of these two tissues are produced. The proportion of phloem to xylem varies in different tree species and under different conditions of growth but is roughly one to five or six. The seasonal ring of phloem is approximately one-fifth as wide as the ring of xylem which is initially formed contemporaneously with it. Finally, trees have developed a method of eliminating old useless phloem tissue through bark sloughing. To sum up, therefore, we may note that wood (xylem) accumulates in a tree because the walls of the cells which compose it are lignified and refuse to crush under bark pressure. Phloem (sap wood) tissues are restricted in amount because —

1. there is less phloem produced than xylem (heart wood);
2. the walls of the sieve tubes of old phloem remain unlignified and crush; and

3. trees cast off old phloem tissues through periderm (cork) formation (*Pls.* 26-28).

Annual rings are evidence of the growth rhythm in trees; the cambium is very active at one season and dormant or sluggish at another. Cold (winter) or dry periods inhibit growth since temperature and moisture are the most potent factors in the activation of the tissue. Trees grow only when climatic conditions permit. Water plays a very important role in the process and growth proceeds most rapidly during hours of darkness. The growing tissue become fluxed with moisture and the growth is hastened thereby. Besides this, there are many more reasons for their appearance. The annual rings could also appear due to the alignment of the pores in a row or in a band of rows beside the distribution of parenchyma in a ring. There is a lot of vacant space in between the cellular, below the fibre saturation point as the walls of the cells consist of several layers; the structure is not very compact physically; it is composed of more than one type of cellular element and hence it is not a homogeneously built substance.

CHEMICAL STRUCTURE

As stated above wood tissue comprises carbon, hydrogen and oxygen. It is assigned a chemical formula of $(C_6H_{10}O_5)$ and is a long chain polymeric compound and a cementing material lignin. The approximate formulae given to them are as shown under which show their chemical structures, their specific material and their properties which are helpful in knowing them better. The cellulose and hemicellulose could be said to form the cellulose armature that is cemented together and made rigid by resinous lignin.

Technique of Making Wooden Objects

In India we have a large range of woods and each region has some specific examples of its own. Selection of wood is a very important step that a carver has to take. The selected wood must possess the smoothness and plasticity desirable for good carving so that the implements can be manipulated as desired. The quality of wood, therefore, is of prime importance to achieve the desired results. Because of this, the early texts on wood carving and for making structures laid down guidelines for selection of wood for a specific purpose.

The *Viṣṇudharmottara Purāṇa*, a text of the sixth century CE says that an architect on an auspicious day enters the forest for selection of trees whose wood would be used for safe results. The trees to be avoided are those with hollows, entwined with creepers, eaten by worms, touched by fire, felled by wind and broken by elephants. The book gives a list of trees which should be avoided. Various other texts like the *Mānasāra*, *Bṛhat-Saṁhitā* of Varāhmihira (seventh century CE), *Bhaviṣya Purāṇa* and *Samarāṅgana Sūtradhāra* datable to the eleventh century CE laid down elaborate rules for selection of wood for making sculptures. It was believed that the quality of the finished product depended upon the quality of wood. After the wood was selected the carving was done. There are two important methods laid down in these scriptures for making a sculpture or an architectural piece:

1. Carving the object from one solid block of wood.
2. Building up the sculpture or the carving from small pieces of wood which were carved out individually and then joined together (*figs.* 8-9).

After a log had dried/seasoned by indigenous techniques, there were two methods for sawing and getting a piece of required dimensions. Sawing it tangentially or sawing it radially were the two methods usually adopted. The radially sawn pieces were found to be more durable than the other. There is a reference of wood joining technique in *Mānasāra,* the ancient Indian treatise on architecture datable to CE 500-700. Several kinds of wood joining techniques are described in detail. Fresh timber should never be joined with pieces of seasoned wood. The ancient people knew that there was no compatibility in them as regards the movements, due to a difference in their structures. Many times bamboo pegs were used for the purpose or pegs of identical wood were used across the grains. It seems that in earlier times painted wooden idols were not favoured. Carvings were so full of minute details that painting would perhaps have spoilt the very purpose of the creation. I had X-rayed five ancient wooden statues to understand their method of wood sculpting and have reported the results in the journal of *Conservation of Cultural Property in India* published by Indian Association for Study of Conservation of Cultural Property in India (vols. XVI-XVII, 1983-84) and found them very useful.

Later on, however, painting of wooden carved designs became a common practice. Painted wooden objects are found after the seventeenth century CE in large numbers and very seldom do we find them intact unless painted on a gesso layer. For display on the occasion of festivals these statues used to be painted again and again by scrubbing the damaged layer. Once, I found seven layers of paint on an image (*Pl.* 29) from Gujarat.

It suggests that it was painted seven times during its lifetime, perhaps when it got damaged and was needed for a festival. In such a case, it was very difficult to identify the exact composition of the various layers since the material being analysed was found to be superimposed by the various layers of repainting.

For polychrome wooden statues two techniques of painting were prevalent in India:

1. Directly on wood without any surface preparation, and
2. With surface preparation.

In the first case the surface of the wood carving or sculpture was smoothened and then a thin coat of paint was applied. The layer of paint was so thin that the grains of wood could still be seen. The paint was prepared by mixing a pigment (red lead, yellow ochre, malachite, iron oxide, lead chromate) with an aqueous medium used for glue. This is mostly true about polychrome statues from south India. In the second case the surface of the wood carving was prepared by applying a coating of gesso to fill the pores and wood grains to make the surface smooth. Gesso was prepared by mixing kaolin, chalk or gypsum with a solution of animal glue. The thickness of the gesso varied from place to place and sometimes it was as thick as 0.5 cm. These results are reported in the journal of *Conservation of Cultural Property in India* (vols. I-V) as a joint study by me and two of my senior colleagues when we worked together in the National Museum, Conservation Department. Mysore paintings being huge in structure were constructed by joining planks to achieve the required size. These planks had a tendency to separate thus forming gaps affecting the painted structure. It also looked very unaesthetic and was a danger to the painting.

Use of paper and cloth was also seen in the layer prepared as a surface for painting. First a cloth was pasted on the surface of the object with glue which made the surface ready to take the gesso layer. In some cases wet paper was applied on the surface to impart smoothness. Before painting, a thin layer of ground was given over the paper. For painting, pigments (red ochre, yellow ochre, malachite, terreverte, ultramarine, lamp black) were mostly mixed with glue solution, or sometimes resin was used. Varnish was invariably used on the painted surface to provide a smooth finish and protection to the paint layer (*fig.* 10). This gave the pigments a necessary tint making them an integral part of the paint. This practice is usually seen in polychrome sculptures from Tamil Nadu. Mysore paintings similarly had a technique of their own.

In Nepal, usually a ground of kaolin was used, and pigments like iron pyrites and oxides, lead chromate, carbon black, ultramarine were mixed with glue and a spirit soluble varnish was applied on the top. Another way of decoration used for the polychrome statues used to be in the form of inlay work. Wood is carved in relief and then inlay patterns are executed. Material used for inlay is mostly ivory, bone, metal or strips of coloured wood. This practice is usually prevalent in north India especially in Kashmir.

Lac work is another example of painted wooden objects. Shellac was used in solution form as a varnish or with a process known as lac-turnery. In the former process, wood was painted and then the shellac varnish was applied with a brush. It gave a lustrous shine to the object. In the lac-turnery work, lac was applied on the object not as a paint or varnish but by heat which is produced due to friction of lac stick on wood. Usually light colour woods are preferred for the lac-turnery work. The wooden object to be lacquered is first polished smoothly or fitted on the lathe and then putty is applied. The next step is to paint the object, for which different colours are used. Sankheda a small town in the state of Gujarat is famous for a very fine golden colour work, by painting the object with a levigated dispersion of tin in glue solution and then applying coloured lac on the top (*fig*. 11).

There is a traditional but special process for the preparation of the tin suspension or solution. Designs are painted by this solution and then polished with a stone. Lac mixed with yellow or red pigment is applied on the surface which results in golden appearance being imparted to the tin painted portions. Coloured lac is prepared by a special process in which the melted lac is mixed with pigment and dispersed in a little oil or water, so that sticks could be made of it. For application of lac on wood, the object is fitted on a lathe. A burning charcoal is kept nearby in a receptacle. The coloured lac stick is placed on the surface of the object which is turned rapidly by the lathe. Due to heat produced by friction, the lac melts and forms a smooth layer over the painted wood. Because the lac is coloured, it changes the colours underneath and provides the wood with a lustrous glowing shine. White tin paint looks like gold work. A light polish in the end finishes the process.

3

Deterioration of Wood

WOODEN objects especially of very ancient past are not available in the same number as they might have been at one time. There are many reasons for their disappearance and as a result of these reasons, we do not find all of them today. Apparently, they may look strong and durable but it is a well established fact that wooden objects are very vulnerable to decay due to various causes and factors natural as well as man-made. The most important factor is their proneness to biological decay both by insects and also by micro-organisms as it is a food for them whenever they grow in a climate favourable for their growth since they thrive on them. During my long tenure of teaching and practical experience of conservation of a large number of wooden objects, I am convinced of their getting damaged quickly. Hot and humid climatic conditions accelerate the multiplication of bio-detergins. Wooden objects are also affected by the changes of RH and temperature, more particularly their rapid and frequent changes. Fire, floods, earthquakes and other natural disasters can also inflict damage resulting in their total loss in no time. In this chapter, deterioration processes affecting artefacts made of wood are grouped into categories: environmental, physical, chemical, mechanical and biological besides the inherent or man-made factors of deterioration. They interact and work together to cause deterioration in both the materials of the object and their structures.

Environmental Degradation

Environment plays a very crucial role in the life of wooden objects.

It constitutes the action of various parameters of the environment namely:

1. humidity;
2. temperature;
3. light;
4. pollution;
5. dirt; etc.

It has been explained earlier in chapter 2 that humid conditions (RH) of the environment play a very crucial role in proportionally changing the moisture content of the wood. This change, therefore, swells the wood substance across the grain when the RH of the environment increases and later when the RH decreases the wood substance shrinks. When the artefact is new the wood substance adapts itself accordingly, but when the object becomes old it cannot cope with the changes. The wood, thus, experiences a lot of stress and strain resulting in changes in dimensions that cause warping, cracking and splitting (*figs.* 12-13).

It is well known that if the capacity to hold water vapour decreases in the surroundings as a decrease of temperature, the wood substance would swell. Conversely, if the capacity of the air to hold water vapour increases wood would shrink. This is a complex problem and needs to be understood more clearly by way of further research as light energy causes thermal degradation at high temperature causing breaking and shortening of the cellulose chain thus making it lose elasticity and become brittle. It involves the absorption of thermal energy by wooden materials. Excitation takes place both within the molecule and the molecule itself resulting in desiccation and shrinkage. Chemical reactions also get accelerated in presence of additional thermal energy. On the other hand, the wooden structures at very low temperature below freezing point would cause repeated freezing and melting of the moisture content of the cell walls alternately if they are exposed to the weather in the open. The wood thus gets weathered, fragile and brittle. The physical condition of wooden objects, therefore, would depend on the environment

1. the objects have met with in the past; and
2. these objects have to face after their entry into a collection.

The forces responsible for decay continue even in the museums and if proper care is not taken, the objects would continue to suffer. It is not proper to think that objects would stop decaying automatically once they are kept in the museum. Instead a proper environmental care has to be ensured. In a tropical climatic environment as that prevalent in India, wooden objects are most prone to decay. Delhi and most parts of north India experience heavy rains during July-September with RH above 60 per cent and temperature rising above 35° C. Likewise during March-June it has a fairly hot climate having an RH below 40 per cent and temperature as high as 42° C. However during October-

February the climate remains favourable and usually does not promote decay since RH and temperature both remain within the prescribed norms.

Intense light and ultraviolet radiations cause photochemical degradation. Lignin an amorphous polymeric substance being poly phenol propane derivative, gets oxidized by ultraviolet radiations. Lignin has an absorption peak at a wavelength of 280nm and extends over 400nm, making it an excellent ultraviolet absorber. Both darkening of light coloured woods and fading of dark coloured woods into light coloured ones is also noticed as these radiations have bleaching properties. The oxidation of oils, resins, dyes and colouring materials in wood takes place because of absorption of light-sensitive, high-energy groups, followed by the formation of largely free radicals, which begin chain oxidation reactions. The oxidation of these materials does have important consequences for wooden materials. The most commonly recognized are the fading, yellowing, darkening of light coloured woods and discolourations of wooden objects in general. Oxidation of the wood results in commonly found changes in permeability, colour, surface gloss, texture, and resistance to abrasion.

Dirt adheres to the wooden artefacts due to both physical and chemical reasons. The primary objective of a conservator is to increase the chemical stability of the object, and cleaning is an important step in the stabilization process. The conservator has to decide judiciously what the final look of the object should be after cleaning so that its aesthetic appearance is maintained, and how much dirt can be tolerated on the object as a historical evidence, etc. without being harmful to the very survival of the object. To me, all the foreign matter which was not part of the object at the time of its fabrication by the artist has to be thinned down to make the details in it clearly visible. Generally, these would be soot, grease-stains, unwanted ugly restoration, if any, besides the decayed surface accumulations and materials which have changed the original look of the object, e.g. yellowed varnish in the case of a painted wooden artefact, which spoil its original beauty (*figs.* 14-15).

Mechanical Degradation

Mechanical process of deterioration results in wear/tear, fractures, abrasions related to deformation, soiling and staining. Mechanical deterioration results in damage that can be understood as interruptions in the original structural continuity intended by the maker. In these cases, specific parts of the structure are damaged and their function within the artefact to absorb and distribute stress to associated structural elements can be lost or impaired. It can take many forms like holes, losses, cuts, chips, dents, accretions such as related to *pūjā* ceremonies, particulate matter of dust, ultimately turning into dirt/grime, and soot. This can also happen from their use and through neglect and improper care. These damages can also be caused due to breakage from stacking or keeping or crowding them in an insufficient space like a small drawer or cabinet and poor exhibition/display techniques. The types of damage that fall into the category of mechanical deterioration are so many that they overlap with other forms of deterioration of wood. Similarly, pollutants attached to particulates can cause acidic deterioration through hydrolysis with available moisture.

Biological Degradation

Deterioration of wood caused by living organisms is called biodeterioration. Biological processes of decay are those which are caused by attacks of fungi, molds, bacteria, insects and rodents. They may result in the weakening of the original materials and structures causing staining, distortion and at times a total loss of details of wood. Wood provides favourable living conditions for the insects and micro-organisms because its cellulose and hemicellulose is a food for them along with the various impurities and water content. The problem is of considerable magnitude in tropical countries like India where the climate is hot and humid for most of the year, and organisms causing biodeterioration flourish in such a weather. Different species of biodeterioration attack different materials:

1. Mice and rats are certainly no strangers for the museum collections and have often made their homes among artefacts. Damage is often in the form of chewing and gnawing marks on the wooden objects, usually with some loss of material. They also leave behind various nesting materials such as chewed up burlap, newspaper and textile rags. Urine and acidic excrement become more harmful sometimes. Moreover, once an egg-bearing female finds suitable conditions to establish a population, artefacts can become a food source for them.
2. Fungi may occur in a wood while it is still alive, when it is dead, when formed into an artefact, while in use, or even when discarded. Thus, fungi may still be active in a storage or display area. The wood decaying fungi can either be a surface mold, sap

stain fungi, decay fungi or a soft rot fungi. Surface mold and sap stain fungi thrive on carbohydrates and do not destroy cellulose or lignin. Brown rot is due to decay-causing fungi which digests only the cellulose and results in its weight loss.

This promotes shrinkage and splits. The fungi hyphae can make holes through cell walls, lie in the cell lumen and digest the cell wall from the lumen onwards. White rot is due to decay-causing fungi which digest only lignin. The loss of lignin causes increased porosity and swelling, resulting in total collapse of the affected area. Soft rot is the decay that occurs in wood with a high moisture content and makes the wood dry and is mostly associated with waterlogged or buried wood. It starts eating the wood from the surface to the inner parts. Soft rot shows preferential decay of late wood cells, causing exfoliation of soft faced growth rings. Dry rot fungi needs wood having a moisture content of 20 per cent and above. It is reported that dry rot usually attacks softwoods and also the sap portion of the hardwoods. Molds cause discolouration on the surface of the wood.

3. Insects are also a very potential source of damage to wooden objects. The most active among them are termites, and wood boring insects such as coleoptera (wood borers), isoptera (termites) (*fig.* 17), hymenoptera (ants, bees and wasps), lepidoptera (moths and wood boring caterpillars) and dictyoptera (cockroaches); (i) furniture beetle (*fig.* 18); (ii) death watch beetle (*fig.* 19); (iii) and powder-post beetle

(*fig.* 20); and (iv) bamboo borer (*fig.* 21) are some other insects which damage wood. In tropics, the main wood destroying insects are the termites which live in colonies. Termites generally reach the wooden materials by means of subterranean galleries. They often hollow the wood completely. All of the beetles which decay wood or wood boring insects, have a life cycle of four stages: egg, larvae, pupa and adult. All of them need a lot of food while the larvae is becoming a pupa. These beetles are mostly hairy, dark brown to black, 3-9 mm long and attack all woods. The powder-post beetles only infest hardwoods. They can be noticed as they leave behind the fine wooden powder. The first two categories of insects stated above make medium size holes but the last two categories, make minute holes. However, termites eat and destroy the wood substance (*figs.* 22-23).

Chemical Degradation

Besides the above-mentioned phenomena, deterioration reactions also take place as a result of inherent, evolved, or introduced chemical compounds. Again, the reactions take place in association with, and sometimes as a result of, other deterioration processes and their byproducts. Reaction to cellulosics, for example, can take place at the margins of crystalline regions, in amorphous regions of cellulose polymer aggregations between micellcs, between aggregations of cellulose polymer in the microfibril, between microfibrils, and fibrils within the cell wall. Hydrolysis is a substantial contributor to deterioration of cellulose and hemicellulose cells at all levels of organization. Finally, the other sources of applied chemical deterioration are the pollutants. Acid makes the wood brittle and the tracheids and fibres become disassociated. Lignin and hemicellulose are degraded by acids and woods lose strength and are softened.

Waterlogging of wood happens if it is submerged under water or wet soil for a long time. It is completely saturated. pH of the soil accelerates decay, making the wood soft like cheese and it loses its mechanical strength. However, it retains its original shape and size so long as it remains in water and buried in the soil. If such an object is removed from the wet soil it starts losing the water so as to maintain equilibrium with the atmospheric RH. If the loss of water is abrupt the cracking would be haphazard not only in the longitudinal direction but vertically also, with the result that there is a complete collapse of the cellular structure. Such wooden objects absorb salts from the soil and are, therefore, salt-laden, fragile and need appropriate treatment. Salt-laden winds from the sea-shore is another problem which is common in wooden structures due to their hygroscopic and tender nature of the carving in them.

In most of the museums the common defect that we find in the painted and varnished wooden objects is invariably the darkening that hides the details underneath. Sometimes the painted wooden objects have flaking of the pigments. In case there are several overlapping layers, it becomes very problematic. It is generally seen that the insects do not like to eat those wooden objects which are polychrome. Whatever is true for the unpainted statues is equally true for the painted statues also except for the biodeterioration aspect. Generally it is observed that insects do not like to eat painted portions but when they attack painted statues they start first with the unpainted portion.

Structural Defects in Wood

Whatever has been discussed in the paragraphs above can be summarized as under:

1. Wood is composed of a complex polymeric material consisting of carbon, hydrogen and oxygen known as cellulose.
2. It is a natural product having directional properties.
3. It is hygroscopic due to polar hydroxyl group (OH) which has an affinity for moisture from water vapour.
4. It undergoes hydrolysis resulting in a shorter chain monomeric material that has lower molecular weight thus converting polysaccharide into monosaccharides and ultimately into sugars.
5. There is a lot of vacant space in between the cellular structure below the fibre saturation point as the walls of the cells consist of several layers.
6. The structure is not compact physically.
7. It is composed of more than one type of cellular elements and hence is not a homogeneously built substance.
8. It has lignin, a cementing material, which gets oxidized due to the photochemical action of light thus losing its binding power/properties due to chemical change.
9. It has directional properties and usually warps and cracks and may split due to changes of RH along

the longitudinal axis and in its volume.

10. Being a carbohydrate, insects and micro-organisms thrive on its cellulose or the cell contents.
11. A stagnant environment promotes the growth of biodetergins.
12. It can easily accumulate dust and particulate matter that turns into dirt and grime.
13. Fungal activity stains the light-coloured woods and rots the wood substance.
14. It is subjected to thermal degradation resulting in weathering.
15. It experiences lots of stress and strain due to the freezing and melting of its water content.
16. Wooden objects may continue to decay in a museum, if after-treatment care is not ensured and collections are not examined regularly for their health care.

Examination and Documentation

Having explained the various aspects of understanding the nature and extent of alterations in the wooden objects, their origin, source, composition, structure, properties, method of making, decay mechanism due to factors like physical, mechanical, chemical, biological, man-made and inherent, are recorded after due scientific examination and documentation have been completed. The examination of the various factors affecting the artefact is completed by using equipment and techniques to record the different aspects of its decay and the present condition. This is documented in the form of textual, graphic and photographic — both visible and invisible radiations — recording of the present condition so as to study and diagnose the defects in a systematic manner to decide about the best possible treatment accordingly. It is needless to mention that we usually use the equipment and technique of examination specific to the different types wood, and also that the results of textual, graphic and photographic documentation are accordingly recorded for future reference.

These findings are recorded first on to a form devised for treatment of wooden objects. Graphic drawings are done and photography by visible as well as by invisible radiations, if any, is completed preferably in colour by a digital camera to get perfect results. All these records are then transferred to an optical disc in a computer for quick retrieval in future for reference. A format of the form is reproduced below (page 49). This aspect has been dealt with by me in detail in my book *Conservation Science* published by Agam Kala Prakashan, Delhi (2003).

I would, here, like to remind the readers that many small laboratories still do not maintain proper records of the objects treated in their units for reasons better known to them. On the basis of my long experience, I can unhesitatingly say that it is always professionally right to keep faithful records that can be referred to in future, but definitely not to be misquoted or misused against the person who did the conservation treatment, because the conservator in question, did his work with all the expertise at his disposal and with the latest equipment available in-house at that point of time. Any short cuts may be disastrous. Conservation, being a job of patience, should not be left to half-baked conservators. It should be conducted under the guidance a person of long experience and only he should

FORMAT

Treatment Record of Wooden Objects

S. No. : Examiner:

Date received : Date of return:

Owner :

Acc. No. :

Brief description :

Provenance :

Period :

Shape & Size :

Number of boards or pieces :

Species of wood :

Condition :

(a) Strength :

(b) Distortion in plane :

(c) Splits :

(d) Biological growth :

Painted/Unpainted :

Nature of paint :

Condition of painting :

Graphic records :

Photographic record :

Negative No. :

(a) Black and white :

(b) X-rays :

(c) Colour :

(d) Macrophotograph :

(e) Slide :

(f) Others :

Scientific analysis (if any) :

Treatment Proposed :

decide whether the job of conservation could be carried out or not. Conservators of long standing and with practical experience should be allowed to handle the curative job of conservation. The documentation ought to be very faithful so that the state of its preservation, the treatment executed step by step and the methods of intervention used could be accurately recorded for the benefit of future conservators.

4

Conservation of Wood

THE aim of conservation has two aspects: the physical which is visible, and the inner significance, or we can say the preservation of the tangible and intangible. To put it in other words, conservation is that which is seen in the object by the general visitor and that which is to be visualized by the conservators. We conservators are, therefore, aiming to conserve it in both its content and spirit. The physical aspect is the conservation, but "how"? This requires the selection of suitable materials and techniques that would best stabilize the object and ensure longevity for it. The metaphysical aspect of conservation is the "why"? This aspect requires that conservators should understand the values hidden in the object so that after his/her intervention is complete, the significance of the artwork both outer and inner is enhanced and not diminished in any way.

As enumerated above in the last chapter we should first complete the task of examination of the object and its documentation so as to describe what is tangible and what is to be understood about the object to gain a complete understanding of the artefact in order to locate all the defects, get acquainted with them and record them by the latest methods available in the format meant for wooden objects. A tentative scheme of conservation steps for the proposed treatment has to be prepared in the form of textual documentation and it should be discussed among the higher departmental conservators to reach a consensus among them on one hand and the curator/director of the collection on the other. The step by step conservation treatments are detailed hereunder.

Steps in Conservation

1. Eradication of the past infection due to insects and micro-organisms by a proper insecticidal and fungicidal treatment;
2. Chemical cleaning after dry cleaning/vacuum cleaning;
3. Consolidation for restoring its present strength;
4. Waterlogged wood;
5. Physical repairs;
6. Restoration; and
7. Preventive Measures.

ERADICATION OF BIODETERIORATION

Fumigation to save the objects from insect attack has been a well-known and effective technique of eradicating infections of the past few decades. This step is vital because of its deep penetration in vapour or gaseous phase. For a successful fumigation, selection of a proper fumigant and the problem of absorption by proteinaceous materials such as wool, furs, leather, etc. is imperative. The fumigation becomes doubly effective under a vacuum. Wooden objects have a lot of vacant space left by the free water after the tree is cut and the wood is sawn from it. The wood tissues die and the wood substance starts losing its water content to maintain equilibrium with the surrounding environment by losing the free water it had earlier when the tree was alive. The fumigant replaces the air and reaches where it normally could not travel under normal circumstances. This is the procedure to kill the active insect attacks or destroy the eggs lying dormant within. Vapour-phase fumigation is most effective and necessary in most of the cases. It is always helpful to recognize the insect attack in its early stages. Such an attack can be detected by simply entering the storage area to detect the smell of stagnant air and a powdery dust beneath the statue or carving. Fumigation in a closed chamber for a week in (50 : 50) carbon tetra chloride and carbon disulphide has been used by many workers with good results. A fumigation chamber is the essential prerequisite for the use of poisonous gases to combat insect infections.

Fumigants such as methyl bromide, hydro-cynic acid and sulfuryl fluoride are used in case of highly affected objects. For general fumigation, para-dichlorobenzene can be used as a repellent in the storage cabinets or in the stores by placing the repellant in small packets in muslin cloth and putting them near the wooden objects. For taking care of the fungal activity, fungicides like thymol may be used for fumigation in an airtight chamber. Thymol does not evaporate at room temperature especially in the winters in India and, therefore, the fumigation chamber should have a heat radiating system at the bottom of the chamber since thymol fumes are lighter than air. For killing the fungal infection we have found it most effective. Spraying of 5 per cent thymol in spirit or a solution of 0.5 penta-chlorophenol can be used on the affected objects directly or indirectly including the storage areas. We should also have the storage areas sprayed with chemicals at intervals where the insects and fungal activity are likely to occur. These fumigants do have their merits and demerits. Perhaps it would be useful for many in the profession to know how the various fumigants work and the number of chemicals that are used as fumigants over the years. As the application of science to conservation advances we notice many new additions to the list of chemicals which professionals started using.

Chemicals like para-dichloro-benzene ($C_6H_4C_{12}$) in solid state at room temperature, carbon-disulphide (CS_2) and carbon-tetra-chloride (CCl_4) in liquid state (1 : 1 or 1 : 3) in a closed chamber being inflammable, thymol crystals ($C_{10}H_{14}O$) at a temperature of 50-60° C and 150 gm/m^3, hydrocynic acid gas (HCN) which is very poisonous, ethylene oxide liquid (CH_2)2O and carbon-di-oxide gas (CO_2) in the ratio of 1 : 9 and is known as carboxide can be used (22 gm/m^3 at 31° C for 5 hrs, ethylene oxide liquid $(CH_2)_2O$ and methyl bromide (CH_3Br) in the ratio of 13 : 87 which is called the Japanese method, methyl bromide (CH_3Br) 30-50 gm/m^3 at 20-30° C for 24 hrs and vikane gas-sulfuryl fluoride (SF_2O_2) and an inert ingredient (alkaline carbonate or bicarbonate) in the ratio of 99 : 1 was being used in the Smithsonian Support Center, Maryland, USA which I visited in the early 1980s.

These days because of the environmental consciousness the use of many chemicals is being discarded and, therefore, the use of chemicals is restricted to a few of them. The recent method is the use of oxygen scavengers which is based on inert atmosphere disinfection by keeping the infected wooden material in ageless low oxygen atmosphere which is lethal to a wide range of insects and their various development stages:

1. The object is sealed in a high barrier plastic laminate with ageless for three weeks at 30° C. The oxygen concentration is reduced to less than 0.05 per cent. By this method, a 100 per cent mortality could be achieved for all insect species.
2. Ageless is described by Mitsubishi Gas Chemical Company, Japan as a chemical oxygen scavenger prepared from powdered iron oxide which rapidly absorbs atmospheric oxygen. It is capable of reducing the oxygen concentration in a closed bag or container and will maintain this level indefinitely depending upon the permeability of the packaging material.
3. It is recommended as an alternative to nitrogen gas packing and described as a safe means of inhibiting aerobic micro-organism growth and as a means of killing insects.
4. Ageless is available in packets and the number of packets to be used would depend upon the size of the object and the air tight plastic bag enclosing the object.

Radiological control or sterile insect technique is another method of getting rid of the biological infection by using Gamma ray radiation from a cobalt 60 source. A dose of cobalt 60 of as low as 5-10 KR reduces the fertility of the male insect by 12 to 75 per cent when used in this technique. Eggs that hatch after the irradiation produce larvae with extensive chromosomal aberrations in the multiplication rate of insects by sterilizing the males, thus making them incapable fertilizing the eggs laid by the females. Thus, the eggs would not hatch. This would check their growth. This has to be done where there is a facility for such a treatment. Ultraviolet rays have been used especially against bacteria and fungi. It is reported that between 275-230 nm ultraviolet rays have a germicidal quality and the best results are achieved at RH values less than 50-60 per cent.

Other procedures of keeping the insects away are the well tested use of materials which are termed as natural biocides or the indigenous methods of keeping the insects away. There are many natural biocides which have a great potential of saving our wooden heritage, making it secure from the insects and micro-organisms. The most widely known and extensively used are neem seeds, neem leaves and turmeric powder. The laboratories which are doing research in the use of plant products can also help us in the field of heritage preservation. We in India are using many indigenous products to keep the bio-activity under control.

CLEANING

The nature and extent of deposits has to be identified first. On its nature and composition would depend the future course of action:

1. Superficial loose accumulations can be taken care of by dry brushing immediately after fumigation or by using a vacuum cleaner gently to improve its look.
2. If the loose deposits have now become grime or dirt, it is possible that it may have gone into the grains of the wooden surface. These, we can thin down from the surface. The details would now be clear and visible. The most important thing to remember is to find a suitable solvent or a mixture of solvents

which would soften the solid grime so as to dislodge it from the scene followed by wiping it off. This must be done immediately after its softening by mechanical means (*figs.* 24-29).

The deposits chemically harmful to the wood substance need special attention. There are some properties of liquids which are very important and have to be known beforehand so that we know what to do and what not to do. One should have the answers for questions like whether the liquid would dissolve the dirt, whether it would damage the wood in any way, whether the liquid has enough penetration or is sticky enough to stay where it is needed, whether the liquid is volatile enough to dry at a reasonable temperature or if it is so volatile that the dirt will be redeposited during cleaning and whether the fumes are toxic and inflammable. The chemical properties decide the solubility and the physical properties such as viscosity and volatility. These can be qualitatively understood in terms of secondary bonding forces between the molecules. However, care has to be ensured that the artefact does not lose its old look after such an operation. A conscious conservation expert needs to know how far to go and when to stop. The aim of a particular treatment should be very clear to the conservator and he should also remember that whatever is being done to the object is well thought of and hence utmost care has to be ensured while treating fragile wood carvings.

CONSOLIDATION

Sometimes wooden objects are so weak because of the attack of fungus and insects that they are in danger of total disintegration/collapse. This makes the wooden artefacts fragile, brittle, disfigured, worm-eaten and tunnelled and, therefore, need consolidation for restoring their structural strength. In a wooden material requiring consolidation, many of the primary and secondary bonds that hold it together have broken to a point where the structure can no longer support its own weight and retain its shape. For these reasons the wood becomes soft and spongy to touch. Consolidation is a way of restoring damages caused that are natural processes. The primary requirement of a consolidant is that it should strongly impregnate the object and bind it together not only in one direction, but in all the three directions, i.e. for the relevant jointing also. A consolidant has to start out in a liquid form and end up as a solid. Although the surface tension determines the extent to which a consolidating liquid penetrates a porous body, other factors affect the rate of penetration. The two main ones are the viscosity of the liquid and the size of the pores.

Selection of a best material for consolidation depends on the individual object, its size and shape as well as on the degree and extent of decay and on the climatic condition where it may be exhibited finally. The selection of a proper consolidator is a very important aspect. Consolidation of a decayed object is a one-time operation and needs careful selection keeping many aspects in mind. The following expression describes the flow of a liquid through a porous body, such as wood.

$$Q = \frac{-KApg\ (\delta h)}{\mu\ (\delta s)}$$

Q = the volume of fluid following per unit of time through a cross-section having an area of A.

μ = the viscosity of the fluid.

p = is the density of the fluid.

g = acceleration due to gravity.

$\delta h/s$ = is the hydrolytic pressure gradient in the direction of flow.

K = is the permeability, a property of the solid material and a measure of the ease with which fluids pass through a porous material.

Since *K* and *A* of a given material cannot be altered and the application of pressure or vacuum is not always feasible, it only leaves the viscosity to be chosen to promote the flow or rate of penetration. Hence *Q* is inversely proportional to the viscosity of the fluid.

1. The consolidator has to reach deep into the structure. This can only be achieved and ensured if it is less viscous as the flow of a liquid through a porous body is indirectly proportional to its viscosity, i.e. less viscous liquids penetrate deep and provide total consolidation but it may not provide physical body substance to the artefact.
2. It is, therefore, necessary to reach a compromise in the case of a highly decayed object since it is preferred by the conservators that the consolidator ensure mechanical/physical strength by filling all the holes, gaps and interspaces of the wood substance now present in a decayed object.
3. The consolidation treatment should not alter the optical look of the treated object.
4. As far as possible the consolidator should help in reducing the thirst for water vapour so as to adjust it during the rapid changes of the RH and temperature.
5. The consolidator should not be a food for insects.
6. Polyvinyl acetate solution.

7. Molten wax and resins in an impregnation chamber under vacuum and low pressure.
8. Wax and resin dissolved in a suitable solvent at low concentration under vacuum and pressure or kept in sun under shade for wax-resin to go deep into the body of the object, i.e. the wood substance. Prior to this, it is necessary to brush or keep the object in the solvent. In the beginning it was thought that we could use infra red lamps so that the wax resin travels inwards (*figs.* 30-33), but it has been reported that IR radiations may degrade the lignin. We may therefore, use solarization as a time tested process which is least harmful.

Weiss (1983) in conclusion reported

> Although wood is a complex material, I believe that many of its micro structural features actually simplified our research. Its anisotropic permeability makes it remarkably similar to one of the theoretical capillary models most frequently discussed in the technical literature on flow in porous media.

WATERLOGGED WOOD

If wooden objects remain submerged under water or wet soil or in marshes for a long time, its cellulose is largely destroyed. pH of the soil accelerates decay, making wood very soft almost like cheese and causes loss of mechanical strength. However, it retains its original shape and size, so long as it remains in water buried in soil; but the evaporation of free water as well as bound water is abrupt which results in widespread cracking. It cracks not only in the longitudinal direction but also across the grains.

There are various processes for the treatment of the water-logged wood. The most important precaution to be taken is to let the waterlogged specimens be submerged till the stabilization technique is ready so that immediately after its removal from the soil it is kept in the stabilizing agent. There are various stabilization methods in use, such as:

1. The alum process in which hot solution of potash alum is used;
2. The alcohol-ether-resin process is another technique in which wood tissue is dried by successively bathing it in stronger solutions of ethyl alcohol and followed by a bath of diethyl ether. The low surface tension of ether minimizes the collapse of cell walls when the ether evaporates. If the resin is dissolved in the final ether bath it will remain in wood;
3. The Deep Freeze drying process replaces the water by tri-methyl carbinol (tertiary butanol) and the wood is then allowed to freeze so as to sublime away the solid tertiary butonol in vacuum;
4. The electrolytic method uses a bath of calcium chloride and sodium silicate solution and a direct current is passed resulting in the precipitation of calcium silicate within the wood substance;
5. Polyethylene glycol 4000 molecular weight is dissolved in distilled water to make a 12 per cent solution in which the waterlogged wooden object is kept so that the PEG travels inside the wood substance wherever there is water and later on the water evaporates and only the PEG in the wood substance remains to hold the tissues together. This treatment could be repeated with a more

concentrated solution of carbo wax as it is called. Two grades of PEG's are reported for the treatment of waterlogged wood, one of lower molecular weight for deep penetration and the other of high molecular weight for stabilizing the highly degraded outer zone of wood. Two charred, wooden artefacts were recovered from the Abric Romani in Capellades (Barcelona, Spain) and indirectly dated to 45,000 years BP by the uranium-thorium method. They have since been treated for preservation and stabilization with polyethylene glycol (PEG 4000) and a setting has been created for them similar to the original so that they may be shown to the public without risk of damage as reported by Anna Jover (1974), in an article "The Application of PEG 4000 for the Preservation of Paleolithic Wooden Artefacts." The cheapest method for conservation of waterlogged wood has been reported by Morgos, Andras and others (1987) by using an unheated sucrose solution. "Consolidation of deteriorated wood by impregnation with soluble thermoplastic resins is considered the most promising method because of their physical and mechanical properties, and their reversibility compared to thermosetting synthetic resins. The type of soluble thermoplastic resin, the type of the solvent, resin concentration, and the drying rate of the solvent were examined in this study to find their effects on the improvement in strength and stiffness. Butvar B98 appears to give somewhat better improvement in strength than Butvar B90. Acryloid B72 has limitations as a consolidator due to solvent retention, the latter acting as a plasticizer.

The choice of solvent or of concentration cannot be made on absolute terms, and must be tailored to the particular requirements and conditions of the object to be treated. Very slow rates of solvent removal after treatment did not appear to be advantageous," as reported by Y. Wang, A.P Schniewind, (1985) in the article "Consolidation of Deteriorated Wood with Soluble resins." Wood, particularly in the presence of excessive moisture, deteriorates due to the action of biological agents and sunlight. Decay manifests itself not only in impairment of physical strength but also in discolouration. Protection of the paint during consolidation by impregnation and polymerization, albeit difficult, is possible. Details of a home-built 23 cm-diameter and 48 cm-long chamber for vacuum impregnation are given. The permeating methyl metha crylate monomer solution used with good results contained bis-4-t-butylcyclohexyl peroxide carbonate as catalyst, and pyridine as activator in addition to methyl metha crylate polymer, which reduced the rate of heat generation by the reaction. Polymerization induced by gamma irradiation also yielded satisfactory results. Case histories of three artefacts are described by Erika Schaffer (Nov. 1974) in a paper on "Consolidation of Painted Wooden Artefacts";

6. Arigal C known as Melamine-formaldehyde is a condensation resin solution of a monomeric compound, which is induced to polymerize within the wood substance by addition of a hardener. These are some of the techniques of treating waterlogged wood. We, at the National Museum in New Delhi

successfully tried out some of these techniques some decades ago on the wood remains found at the ancient site of Pāṭaliputra, the modern Patna; and

7. Radiation polymerization has been used as an alternative to other known methods of polymerization of monomers using radiation.

These monomers are introduced into the wood by a solvent exchange process, replacing the water by methanol and the methanol by a monomer. In this case, of the water-soluble monomer 2-hydroxyethyl metha crylate, only one exchange process would be needed. After complete diffusion, the wood monomer combination is irradiated by gamma radiation from a cobalt 60 source. There are many advantages to this method as reported by Munnikendam (1967) such as greater diffusion coefficients of the monomer with an easy penetration in the intra molecular spaces of the cell wall. Moreover, it is not hazardous. The bulking material increases the strength of the wood and gamma radiations penetrate very deep so as to polymerize every part of the wood.

Other successful methods described, and in use in most of the institutes are reported above. Along with these and on the basis of literature survey it can be concluded that the polyethylene glycol (PEG) method, the sucrose method, the acetone-rosin method, the freeze drying method and the silicone oil treatment are some of the methods that are being used in most of the laboratories the world over. Perhaps, we should realize that each method has its merits and demerits to suit individual needs. We should continue to improve our treatment procedures in the interest of conservation and in order to combat post-treatment problems in the form of incomplete curing, residual solvents, ageing of the consolidates making them irreversible, the after-effects of impurities from the manufacturing process or additives, sweating of consolidates and the attack on them by biological pests.

PHYSICAL REPAIRS

The above described methods of consolidation can be supplemented by mechanical reinforcement by using wood of the same species. Alternately, saw dust mixed with fevicol, Paraloid B72 with saw dust and Araldite AV121 have been used to fill the gaps and losses. The large gaps and losses are first filled with wooden pieces of the exact size of the gap, especially made by a wood restorer and joined by using fevicol to the main body of the statue and the remaining gaps being filled by using the mixture of saw dust and fevicol in a PVA emulsion. A few decades back, I experimented on conservation problems of wooden objects with reference to consolidation. These experiments are reported in one of my publications in the *Conservation of Cultural Property in India*, vol. VII, 1974 in which I tried the consolidation of ten fresh samples of wood and tabulated the results. These were conducted with wax and resin dissolved in turpentine and spirit and it was found that in a fixed period from 1 per cent to 9 per cent by weight of dry samples could be introduced. Since then, many other consolidates have come in the market which need to be evaluated accordingly. They can be imported from abroad as our economy has opened up now.

Impregnation with different materials has been attempted abroad by using:

1. Xylamon-LX-hardening;

2. Monomers of vinyl acetate or methyl metha crylate;
3. Polyester resins;
4. Epoxy pre-polymers;
5. Araldite 19, Hardner HY219, Accelerator DY219;
6. Araldite SV426 (coloured) with phenol resin micro-balloons and hardener;
7. Araldite XN 1023(white) with glass micro balloons and hardener;
8. Low viscosity epoxy resins such as Araldite BY158, Hardener HY 22996 which remain fluid for a longer duration. Artificial resin solutions of medium density (20-30 per cent) in high boiling white spirit) and Mowilith 30, 20 per cent dissolved in toluene. There are some ready made products like Lignol AS/AW-K which is used as a filler. There are some monomers which are allowed to polymerize by the use of chemical catalysts. Use of wood consolidators dissolved in organic solvents including acrylic resins with a suitable hardener has been reported from abroad. Joining of the splits and broken parts can be done by using fevicol (polyvinyl acetate emulsion) and filling of the lacunae with a putty of kaolin mixed with Fevicol (*figs*. 34-35).

The most useful publication on the full range of aesthetic compensation materials for wood remains R. Barclay and D.W. Grattan's paper (1988), "A Silicone Rubber/Micro Balloon Mixture for Gap-filling in Wooden Objects." Because of the wide range of materials covered in that paper, the issue of structural compensation was not treated in great depth. This article focuses on philosophy, materials, and techniques used today by wood conservators when structural (weight-bearing and shear-resisting) compensation is required. Aesthetic fill material is not necessarily dependent upon specific compatibility with the substrate material, so the range of choice of materials can be quite wide. However, since material and strength compatibilities are critical to a structural fill, those applied to wood objects fall within a fairly small range. Literature on the subject is limited, and practices among wood conservators are relatively uniform: use of wood fills, thermosetting synthetic fills, and combinations of the two has been reported by Michael S. Padmaniczky in an article (1998) on "Structural fills for Wood Objects: Contrasting and Comple-mentary Approaches."

RESTORATION/RETOUCHING

When it comes to retouching, it can be done by using water-soluble colours matching as far as decided as a policy, keeping the structure, texture and optical appearance in mind. It should not attract the attention of the viewer at first glance, since the details of the objects are more important than the restored parts. Sometimes a statue may be so damaged at the bottom or on the other sides, that it may need some suitable protection to control the damage further. In such cases it can be kept in a specially made wood enclosure so as to fit the statue loosely in it by using fevicol as an adhesive and process of retouching as mentioned above can be repeated to take care of the gaps. This would not only ensure their safety but would also maintain their aesthetic look (*figs.* 36-37) to the liking of the experts in the heritage study.

PREVENTIVE MEASURES

We ought not to relax in any way after the wooden objects have been treated in a conservation laboratory thinking that they would not need any further care. As a matter of fact, continuously provided care is the best preventive measure of conservation to safeguard the objects from the decay process which may be active in a museum even now. These preventive measures would protect them for posterity as described in the various chapters of this book for the control of the various parameters of environment and what is to be done, besides what is not to be done. The ultimate survival would depend on the care the artefacts would receive by way of preventive as well as curative conservation. We should realize here that only those artefacts could survive up to the point of their entry in a collection which had some form of maintenance as the rest were lost due to lack of proper care.

There are many safety measures which need to be taken regarding the operators while treating the wooden objects, especially, while using them for the fumigation of wooden objects. The disposal of the used fumigants from the fumigation chamber must be controlled. Adequate safety precautions must be ensured by the persons handling the work, and last but not the least any potential deleterious effects of the fumigants on the objects must be taken into account. This knowledge of and sensibility to each of these components has increased resulting, thereby, in restricting the choice.

Bibliography

Abdurahem, K., "Insect Pests of Wooden Objects and Their Control," Conservation of Cultural Property in India, vol. 30 (1997), pp. 45-51.

Agarawala, R.C., "Unpublished Katarmal Wooden Reliefs in the National Museum, New Delhi and Connected Problems," *East and West*, vol. 17, nos. 1-2 (March-June, 1967), pp. 83-95.

Agarwal, O.P., *Care and Preservation of Museum Objects*, National Research Laboratory for Conservation of Cultural Property, Lucknow, 1977.

———, "Technique of Wood Work In India," Proceedings of the International Symposium on the Conservation and Restoration of Cultural Property, 1978, Tokyo National Research Institute of Cultural Properties, Tokyo, pp. 77-85.

Agarwal, O.P. and A.S. Bisht, "Technical examination and conservation of a wooden object," *Studies in Museology*, 4 (1968), pp. 55-58.

———, "Anatomical Study of Wood Samples from Art Objects," *Conservation of Cultural Property in India* (*Prof. G.N. Pant Commemoration Volume*), eds. A.S. Bisht, I.K. Bhatnagar and S.P. Singh, Agam Kala Prakashan, Delhi, vol. I-V (2000) pp. 119-23.

Agarwal, O.P. and Shashi Dhawan, (eds.), "Biodeterioration of Cultural Property," Proceedings of the International Conference, held at the NRLCP (February 20-25, 1989), Lucknow, India, Macmillan India Limited, Delhi.

Agarwal, O.P., B.N. Tandon and A.S. Bisht, "A Study of Four Polychrome Sculptures," *Conservation of Cultural Property in India (Prof. G.N. Pant Commemoration Volume)*, eds. A. S. Bisht, I.K. Bhatnagar and S.P. Singh, Agam Kala Prakashan, Delhi, vol. I-V (2000), pp. 169-76.

Ambrose, W., "Freeze Drying of swamp degraded wood," IIC Conference on the Conservation of Stone and Wood, New York, 1970, pp. 53-57.

———, *Stabilizing Degraded Swamp Wood*, ICOM Committee for Conservation, 4th Triennial Meeting Venice, 1975.

Anon, "Two PEGs are Better than One," *Chemistry in Britain*, vol. 23 no. 5 (May 1987), p. 412.

Argyropoulos, V., C. Degrigny and E. Guilminot, "Monitoring Treatments of Waterlogged Iron-wood Composite Artefacts using Hostac or IT-PEG 400 Solutions," *Studies in Conservation*, vol. 45, no. 4, (2000), pp. 253-64.

Barclay, R.L. and D.W. Grattan, "A Silicone Rubber/Microball on Mixture for Gap Filling in Wooden Objects," Proceedings of ICOM Committee for Conservation, 8th Triennial Meeting, Sydney, 1987, vol. 1, pp. 183-87.

Batra, N.L., "Conservation of Wooden Edifices and Artefacts," *Conservation of Cultural Property in India*, vol. 28 (1995), pp. 136-44.

Bhatia, S.K. "Conservation of Waterlogged Wood," Technical Note. 3, NRLC, Lucknow, (1998), pp. 1-16.

Bhatnagar, I.K. and G.I.A. Prabhkaran, "Conservation of wooden carvings in Karanji Mansion, Mysore," *Conservation of Cultural Property in India*, vol. 22 (1989), pp. 19-20.

Bhatnagar, I.K., "Conservation of Temple Ratha: Problems and Suggestions," *Conservation of Cultural Property in India*, vol. 18-20 (1985-87), pp. 102-04.

Bhowmik, S., "Conservation of a Wooden Sculpture from the Baroda Museum," *Baroda Museum and Picture Gallery, Bulletin*, vol. 19, (1965-66), pp. 66-69.

Bisht, A.S., "Conservation of Ethnographic Collections in Museums with Special Reference to Wooden Artefacts," *Conservation of Cultural Property in India*, vols. 18-20 (1985-87), pp. 48-53.

———, "Conservation of Decayed Wooden Objects," in *Conservation of Cultural Property in India*, vol. VII (1974), pp. 47-49.

———, "Conservation Problems of Wooden Cultural Property in the National Museum, New Delhi," Proceedings of the International Symposium on the Conservation and Restoration of Cultural Property, 1983, Tokyo National Institute of Cultural Properties, Tokyo, pp. 93-105.

———, "Prevention and Eradication of Biodeterioration in Museums — A Study of Problems and Future Prospects," *Journal of Indian Museums*, vol. XLIII, 1987, pp. 163-68.

———, "Radiology of Some Painted Wooden Objects: A Preliminary Study," *Conservation of Cultural Property in India*, vols. 16-17, (1983-84), pp. 40-44.

———, *Scientific Aspects of Heritage Study*, Agam Kala Prakashan, Delhi, 2004.

Bjordal, C.G. and T. Nilsson, "Observations on Microbial Growth during Conservation Treatment of waterlogged Archaeological Wood," *Studies in Conservation*, vol. 46, no. 3 (2001), pp. 211-20.

Blanchetta, Robert A., Per Hoffmann, "Degradation Processes in Waterlogged Archaeological Wood," Proceedings of the fifth ICOM Group on Wet Organic Materials Conference, Portland, Maine, 1993, ICOM Committee For Conservation, Working Group on Wet Organic Archaeological Materials (1994).

Brokerhof, Agnes W., "Solarization: A cheap but Effective Method to Disinfect Museum Objects," *Preprints of the ICOM Committee for Conservation*, vol. I, 2002, pp. 15-20.

Brommelle, N.S. (ed.), *Conservation of Wood in Paintings and Decorative Arts*, International Institute of Conservation, London (1987).

Brown, H.P., *An Elementary Manual on Indian Wood Technology*, Govt. of India, Central Publication Branch, Kolkata, 1925.

Caple, Chris and Will Murray, "Characterization of a Waterlogged Charred Wood and Development of a Conservation Treatment," *Studies in Conservation*, vol. 39, no. 1, (February 1994), pp. 28-38.

Carlson, S.M. and A.P. Schniewind, "Residual Solvents in Wood-Consolidant Composites," *Studies in Conservation*, vol. 35, no. 1 (February 1990), pp. 26-32.

Chaudhury K.A.N. and S.S. Ghosh, "Plant Remains from Hastinapura," *Ancient India*, nos. 10-11 (1954-55), pp. 120-38.

———, "Wood Remains from Shishupal Garh," *Ancient India*, vol. 8 (1952) pp. 28-32.

———, "Plant Remains from Harappa," *Ancient India*, no. 7 (1951).

Chaudhary, K.A., "Aspects and Appraisal of Indian Palaeobotany," 1974, pp. 665-71.

Cook, T., *Flora of Bombay*, Botanical Survey of India, Kolkata, vol. II, p. 504.

Deshpande, M.N., "Important Epigraphic Records from Caitya Cave, Bhaja," *Lalit Kala*, 6, October (1959), pp. 20-32.

Devi, K. Indrani, "Conservation of Waterlogged Wooden Canoe — A case Study," *Conservation of Cultural Property in India*, vol. 30 (1997), pp. 9-13.

Devkar, V.L., "History and Preservation of Wood Carvings in Gujarat," *Conservation of Cultural Property in India*, vol. 22 (1989), pp. 21-23.

Dhawan, Shashi, "Identification of Wood of Bhuta Figures of Crafts Museum, New Delhi," *Conservation of Cultural Property in India*, vols. 18-20 (1985-87), pp. 54-56.

Emilio Margeno et al., "A Method for Monitoring the Surface Conservation of Wooden Objects by Raman Spectroscopy and Multivariate Control Charts," *Analytical Chemistry*, vol. 75 no. 20 (2003), pp. 5567-574.

Fielden, Bernard M., *Conservation of Historic Buildings*, Butterworth Scientific Series, 1982.

Gairola, T.R., *Handbook of Chemical Conservation of Museum Objects*, M.S. University of Baroda, Dept. of Museology (1960), p. 101.

———, "Preservation of Wooden Antiquities," *Journal of Indian Museums*, vol. VII (1951), pp. 25-35.

———, "Restoration and Preservation of Archaeological Museum Exhibits," *Journal of Indian Museums*, vol. V (1949), p. 34.

Gallene, *Science for Conservators: Adhesives and Coatings*, Museum Technology (1992).

Gamble, J.S., *A Manual of Indian Timbers*, Bishan Singh Mahendra Pal Singh, Dehradun, (1972) Timber Research and Development Association, Pitman Press, Great Britain.

———, *Flora of Presidency of Madras*, vol. I, pp. 120, vol. III, pp. 952-56.

Garg, K.L. and Shashi Dhawan, "Microbial Deterioration of Wooden Cultural Property," *Conservation of Cultural Property in India*, vol. 18-20 (1985-87), pp. 74-85.

Garg, K.L., Neelima Garg, K.G. Mukherji, *Biodeterioration of Cultural Heritage*, Kolkata, 1994.

Gayathri, P., "Use of Styrofoam in Consolidation of Wooden Antiquities," *Conservation of Cultural Property in India*, vol. 22 (1989), pp. 24-26.

Ghosh, S.S., and Krishna Lal, "Plant remains from Rangpur," *Ancient India*, vol. 18-19 (1962-63), pp. 161-75.

Gilberg, Mark and Alex Roach, "The Effects of Low Oxygen Atmospheres on the Powder Post Beetle, Lyctus brunneus (Stephens)," *Studies in Conservation*, vol. 38, no. 2 (May 1993), pp. 128-32.

Gilberg, Mark, "Inert Atmosphere Fumigation of Museum Objects," *Studies in Conservation*, vol. 34, no. 2 (May 1989), pp. 80-84.

———, "The Effects of Low Oxygen Atmospheres on Museum objects," *Studies in Conservation*, vol. 36, no. 2 (May 1991), pp. 93-98.

Grattan, D.W. and R.L. Barclay, "A Study of Gap-fillers for Wooden Objects," *Studies in Conservation*, vol. 33, no. 2 (May 1988), pp. 71-86.

Grattan, David W. and Mark Gilberg, "Ageless Oxygen Absorber: Chemical and Physical Properties," *Studies in Conservation*, vol. 39, no. 3 (Aug. 1994), pp. 210-14.

Grattan, David, W., ed., *Proceedings of the ICOM Waterlogged Wood Working Group*, Working Group Committee for Conservation, ICOM, Ottawa, 15-18 September 1981, Canadian Conservation Institute Ottawa (1982).

Gupta, C.B., "Deterioration and Conservation of Wooden objects," *Conservation of Cultural Property in India*, vol. 30 (1997), pp. 14-20.

Harinarayana, N., "Conservation of Wood Carvings in the Government Museum, Madras," *Conservation of Cultural Property in India*, vol. 7 (1974), pp. 50-51.

Higuchi, Seiji, "Consolidation and Restoration of Deteriorated Wooden Materials with Synthetic Resins," Proceedings of the International Symposium on the Conservation and Restoration of Cultural Property in The Conservation of Wooden Cultural Property, 1983, Tokyo National Research Institute of Cultural Properties, Tokyo, pp. 23-32.

Iwasaki, Tomokichi, "Basic Consideration of Conservation and Restoration of Cultural Property," International Symposium on the Conservation and Restoration of Cultural property, (1979) — Conservation of Far Eastern Art Objects, Tokyo National Research Institute of Cultural Properties, 1980, pp. 181-86.

Johnson, Colin, Kerry Head and Lorna Green, "The Conservation of a Polychrome Egyptian Coffin," *Studies in Conservation*, vol. 40, no. 2 (May 1995), pp. 73-82.

Jong, J. de., "The Conservation of Shipwrecks," in Proceedings of the ICOM Committee for Conservation, 5th Triennial Meeting, Zagreb, 1978.

Jover, Anna, "The Application of PEG 4000 for the Preservation of Paleolithic Wooden Artefacts," *Studies in Conservation*, vol. 39 no. 3 (August 1994), pp. 193-98.

Kaye, Barry, David J. Cole-Hamilton, and Kathryn Morphet, "Supercritical Drying: A New Method for Conserving Waterlogged Archaeological Materials," *Studies in Conservation*, vol. 45, no. 4 (2000), pp. 233-52.

Kuhn, Herman, *Conservation and Restoration of Works of Art and Antiquities*, vol. I (1986), Butterworths, London.

Lan, Zhang, "A Note on the Conservation of a Thousand Year Old Boat," *Studies in Conservation*, vol. 40, no. 3 (August 1995), pp. 189-93.

Mangiraj, V.R., R.S. Trimbake and K.K. Swarnkar, "Conservation of Wooden Polychrome Sculptures," *Conservation of Cultural Property in India*, vols. 30 (1997), pp. 40-44.

McCawley, J.C., "Waterlogged Artefacts: The Challenge to Conservation," *Canadian Conservation Institute Journal*, vol. 2 (1977), pp. 17-36.

Mckay, W.B., Building Constructions, vol. I, Longmans, London (1945).

Mittre, Vishnu and H.P. Gupta, "Plant Remains from Ancient Bhatkuli, District Amaraoti, Maharastra," *Puratattva*, vol. 2 (1968-69), pp. 21-22.

Moncrieff, Anne, "Review of Recent Literature on Wood (January 60-April 68), *Studies in Conservation*, vol. 13, no. 4 (1968), pp. 186-212.

Morgos, Andras and others, "The Cheapest Method for Conservation of Waterlogged Wood: The Use of Unheated Sucrose Solutions," ICOM Committee for Conservation: 8th Triennial Meeting Sydney, 1987, pp. 313-19.

Mori, Hachiro and Hideo Arai, "Biodeterioration of Wooden Cultural Properties and its Control," Proceedings of the International Symposium on the Conservation and Restoration of Cultural Property — Conservation of Wood, 1978, Tokyo

National Research Institute of Cultural Properties, Tokyo, pp. 1-16.

Muhlethaler, Bruno et al., *Conservation of Waterlogged Wood and Wet Leather*, ICCROM, ROME, 1971, p. 71.

Müller-Beck, H. and A. Haas, "A Method for Wood Preservation using Arigal C," *Studies in Conservation*, vol. 5 (1960), pp. 150-57.

Mumikandam, R.A., "Conservation of Waterlogged Wood using Radiation Polymerization," *Studies in Conservation*, vol. 12 (1967), pp. 70-75.

———, "Low Molecular Weight Epoxy Resins for the Consolidation of Decayed Wooden Objects," *Studies in Conservation*, vol. 17 (1972), pp. 202-04.

Nair, G.S., "Preservation of a Wooden Object from Nepal," *Journal of Indian Museums*, vols. 17-20, (1961-64), pp. 61-63.

Nair, S.M., "Some Simple Methods for Examination of Organic Objects under Insect Attack," *Conservation of Cultural Property in India*, vol. 11 (1978), pp. 29-30.

Nakhla, S.M., "A Comparative Study of Resins for Consolidation of Wooden Objects," *Studies in Conservation*, vol. 31 (1986), pp. 38-44.

Organ, R.M., "Carbowax and other Materials in the Treatment of Waterlogged Paleolithic Wood," *Studies in Conservation*, vol. 4 (1959), pp. 96-105.

———, "Limitations in the Use of Polyethylene Glycol," *Studies in Conservation*, vol. 5 (1960), pp. 161-62.

Pacard, E., Consolidation of Decayed Wood Sculpture," *Conservation of Stone and Wooden Objects*, (Wooden Section), IIC, London, 1970, pp. 13-22.

Parikh, R.T., "Lacquer Industry of Sankheda (Gujarat)," *Journal of Indian Museums*, vol. 29 (1973), pp. 88-93.

Pearson, C., ed., *Waterlogged Wood in Conservation of Marine Archaeological Objects*, 1987, pp. 55-87 and 164-206, Butterworths, London.

Plenderlieth, H.J., *The Conservation of Antiquities and Works of Arts*, Oxford University Press, London, (1956), pp. 127-29.

Plenderlith, H.J. and A.E.A. Werner, *The Conservation of Antiquities and Works of Art*, 2nd edn., 1929, Oxford University Press, London.

Rao, K.R. and K.B.S. Juneja, *A Handbook for Field Identification of Fifty Important Timbers of India*, Forest Research Institute and Colleges, Dehradun Press, 1971.

Ray, M. Seborg and Robert B. Inverarity, "Conservation of 200 year old Waterlogged Boats with Polyethylene Glycol," *Studies in Conservation*, vol. 7 no. 4 (November 1962), pp. 111-20.

Rosenquist, A.M., "Stabilizing of Wood Found in the Viking Ship of Oseburg," Part I, *Studies in Conservation*, 4 (1959), pp. 13-22.

———, "Stabilizing of Wood Found in the Viking Ship of Oseburg, Part II," *Studies in Conservation*, 4 (1959), pp. 62-72.

Santhakumaran, L.N. and M.V. Rao, "Natural Durability of Some Common Members and Marine Plywood against Biodeterioration in Kochi Waters," *Journal of the Timber Development Association of India*, vol. 40, no. 1 (1994), pp. 40-53.

Sawada, Masaaki, "Conservation of Waterlogged Wooden Materials from the Nara Palace Site," *Proceedings of the International Symposium on the Conservation and Restoration of Cultural Property* — Conservation of Wood, 1977, Tokyo National Research Institute of Cultural Properties, pp. 49-58.

Schaffer, E., "Conservation of Soft Wood Artefacts," *Studies in Conservation*, 16 (1971), pp. 110-13.

Sebrorg, R.M. and R.B. Inverarity, "Conservation of 200 Year Old Waterlogged Boats with PEG," *Studies in Conservation*, vol. 7 (1962), pp. 111-19.

Shah, A.R., "Application of Cashew Nut Oil as Wood Preservative," *Conservation of Cultural Property in India*, vol. 23 (1990), pp. 28-29.

Shaheen, Fauzia, "Insect Factor in Deterioration of Wooden Cultural Property," *Conservation of Cultural Property in India*, vols. 18-20 (1985-87), pp. 62-70.

Sharma, B.R.N., "Chemical Treatment and Preservation of Wooden Ter Gate," *Conservation of Cultural Property in India (Prof. G.N. Pant Commemoration Volume)*, eds., A.S. Bisht, I.K. Bhatnagar and S.P. Singh, Agam Kala Prakashan, Delhi, vols. I-V (2000), pp. 136-37.

Simunkova, E., Z. Smejkalova, and J. Zelininger, "Consolidation of Wood by the Method of Monomer Polymerization in the Object," *Studies in Conservation*, vol. 28 (1983), pp. 133-44.

Sreelatha Rao and G. Kamlakar, "Wooden Beams and Rafters on the Durbar Hall, Golkonda Fort," *Conservation of Cultural Property in India*, vol. 30 (1997), pp. 1-8.

Stark, Barbara L., "Waterlogged Wood Preservation with PEG," *Studies in Conservation*, vol. 21 (1976), pp. 154-58.

Talwar, M.S., "Preservation of Waterlogged Wood of Mauryan Period," *Conservation of Cultural Property in India (Prof. G.N. Pant Commemoration Volume)*, eds., A.S. Bisht, I.K. Bhatnagar and S.P. Singh, Agam Kala Prakashan, Delhi, vols. I-V (2000), pp. 256-57.

Tandon, B.N., "Few Wooden Polychromes of 19th Century, Their Scientific Study," *Conservation of Cultural Property in India*, vol. 8 (1975), pp. 35-37.

———, "Four Wooden Polychromes of 19th Century: Their Scientific study," *Conservation of Cultural Property in India*, vol. 8 (1997), pp. 35-37.

Thomson, G., ed., *Recent Advances in Conservation*, Butterworths, London, 1963.

Thomson, Garry, "Preprints for the Contribution to the New York Conference," *Conservation of Stone and Wooden Objects*, IIC, London, vol. II, 1972.

Toishi, Kenzo, "Cracking and Deformation of Wooden Objects," *Proceedings of the International Symposium on the Conservation and Restoration of Cultural Property*, (1979), Conservation of Far Eastern Art Objects, Tokyo National Research Institute of Cultural Properties, 1980, pp. 133-48.

———, "Conservation of Organic Museum Objects in Japan," *Studies in Museology*, vol. 10 (1975-76), pp. 79-90.

Trotter, H., *The Common Timbers of India and Their Uses*, Publication Division, Govt. of India, 1959, pp. 199, 229-30 & 263-82.

Tsujimoto, Kan'ya, "On My Five Years Experience of Repairs of Wooden Statues in the United States," Proceedings of the International Symposium on the Conservation and Restoration of Cultural Property, (1979) — Conservation of Far Eastern Art Objects, Tokyo National Research Institute of Cultural Properties, 1980, pp. 125-32.

Unger, Achim, Schniewind, W. Unger, *Conservation of Wood Artefacts: A Handbook*, Springer-Verlag, Berlin, Germany (2001).

Valentin, Nieves, Mary Lindstrom and Frank Preusser," "Microbial Control by Low Oxygen and Low Humidity environment," *Studies in Conservation*, vol. 35, no. 4 (November 1990), pp. 222-30.

Vishnudharmottara Purana, ed. P.B. Shah (G.O. Series) Baroda 1961, Khaṇḍa III, Chapter 89, pp. 194.

Wang, Y. and Schniewind, A.P., "Consolidation of Deteriorated Wood with Soluble Resins," *Journal of the American Institute for Conservation*, vol. 24, no. 2 (Spring 1985), pp. 77-91.

Ward, Clare, Derrick Giles, Dean Sully and David John Lee, "The Conservation of a Group of Waterlogged Neolithic Bark Bowls," *Studies in Conservation*, vol. 41, no. 41 (1996), pp. 241-49.

Watson, J., "The Application of Freeze-Drying on British Hardwoods from Archaeological Excavations," *Proceedings of the ICOM-Waterlogged Wood, Working Group Conference*, ed. D. W. Grattan, Committee for Conservation, 1982, pp. 237-42.

Weaver, Martin E., "Successes and Failures in the Conservation of Wooden Structures," *Journal of Architectural Conservation*, vol. 9, no. 3 (2003), pp. 36-50.

Weiss, Norman R., "Three Research Problems," *Proceedings ISCRP,* Wood Conservation (1983), pp. 287-95.

Werner, A.E., "Consolidation of Deteriorated Artefacts," *Proceedings of the International Symposium on the Conservation and Restoration of Cultural Property* — Conservation of Wood, Tokyo National Research Institute of Cultural Properties (1978), pp. 17-21.

———, "Consolidation of Fragile Objects — Waterlogged Wood," *Studies in Conservation,* vol. 6, no. 4 (November 1961), pp. 133-34.

Wheeler, R.E.M., "Harappa 1946: The Defenses and Cemetery R 37," *Ancient India,* no. 3 (1947), pp. 59-130.

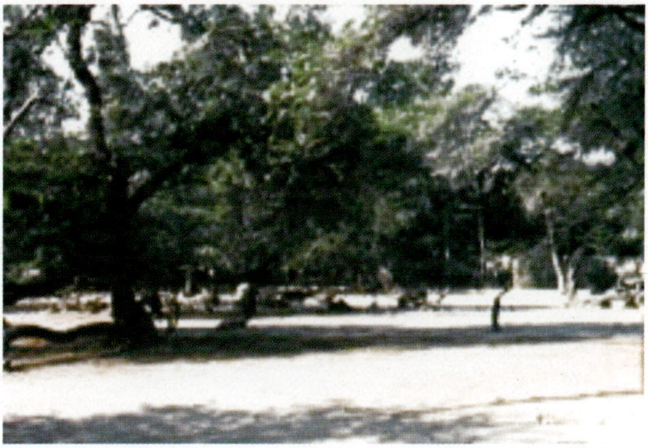

Pl. 1: Natural forests in Uttarakhand

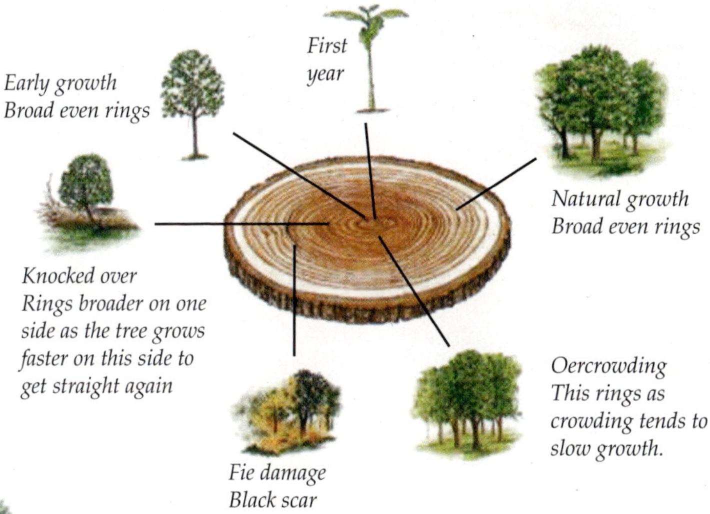

Pl. 2: Growth of trees — An artistic vision

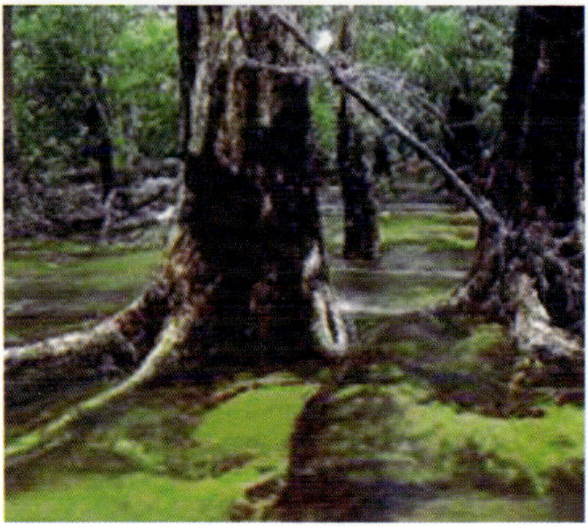

Pl. 3: Trees bind the soil

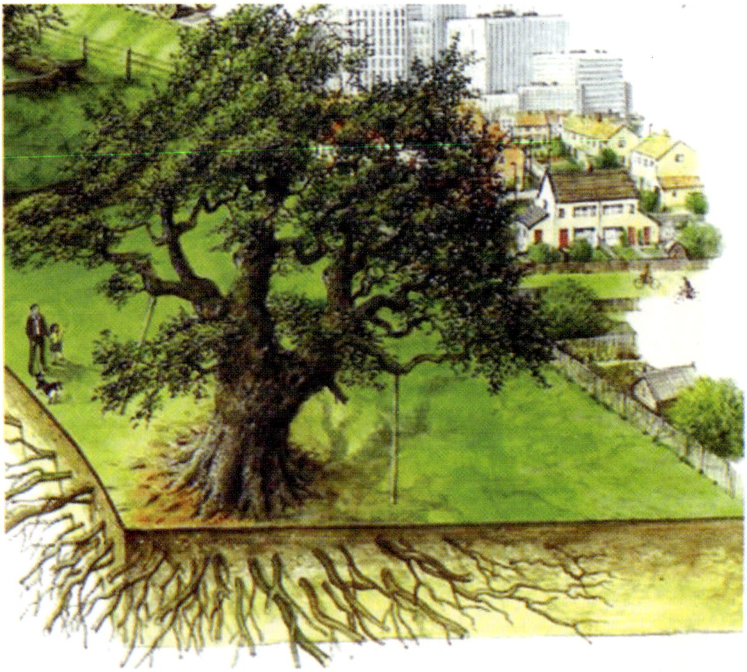

Pl. 4: Roots help trees from rain and floods

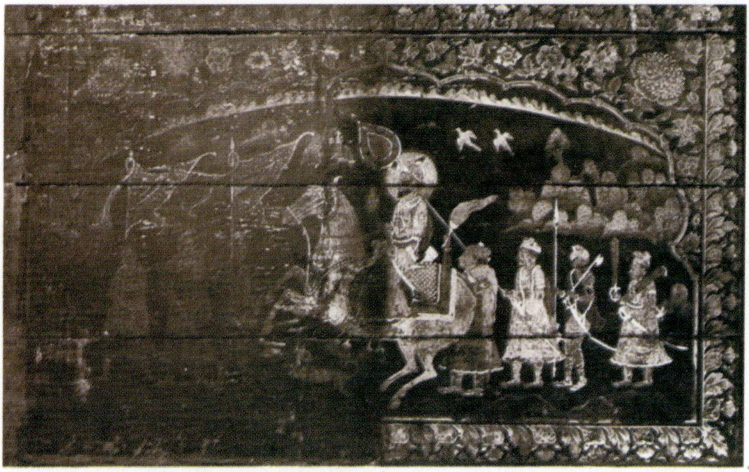

Pl. 5: Pahari Painting on wood during treatment

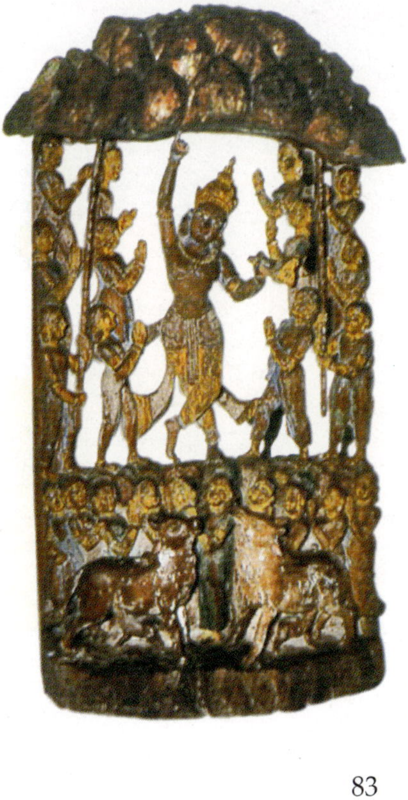

Pl. 6: Painted wooden statue of Goverdhandhārī Kṛṣṇa

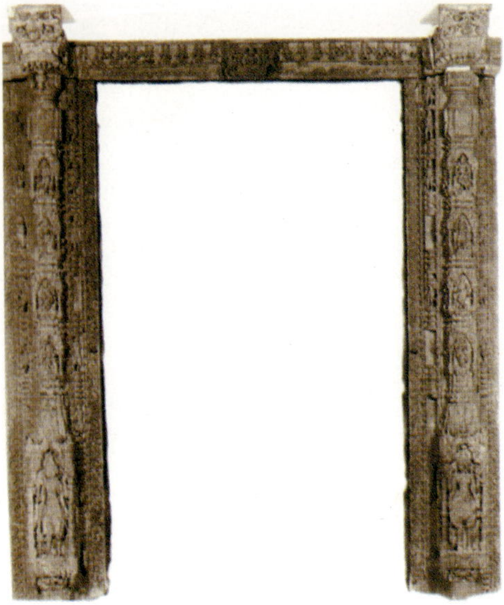

Pl. 7: Wooden doorway from Gujarat

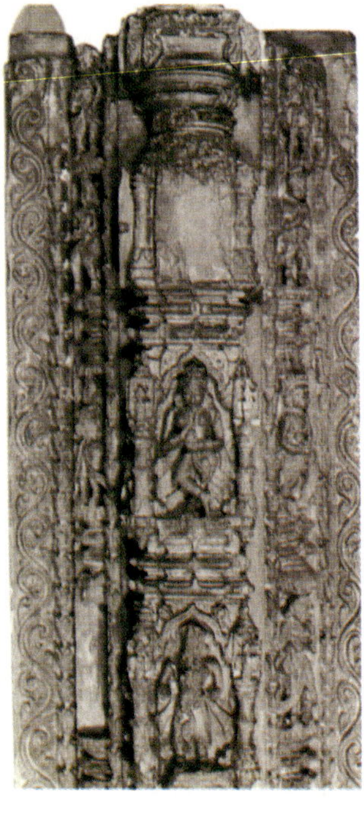

Pl. 8: Details of a portion of wooden doorway from Gujarat

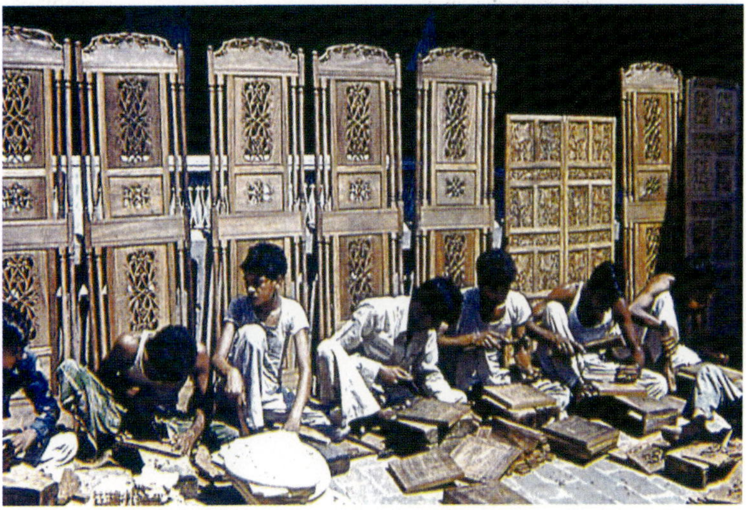

Pl. 9: Craftsmen at work

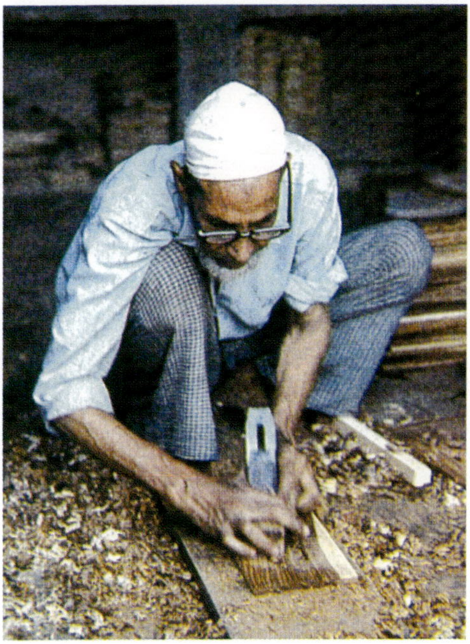

Pl. 10: Master craftsman at work

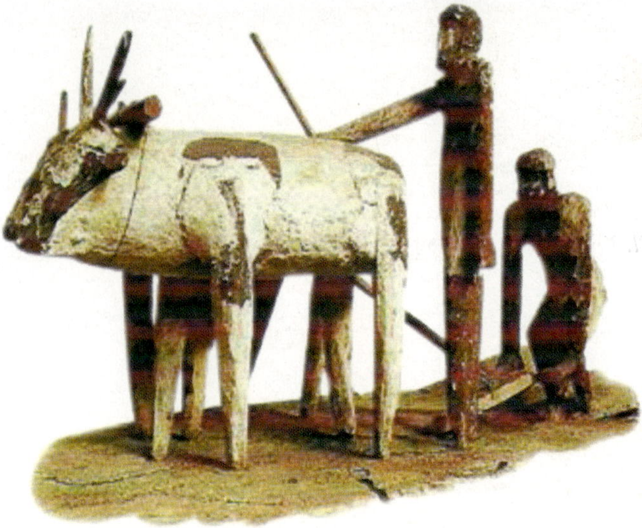

Pl. 11: Wooden statue showing early farming

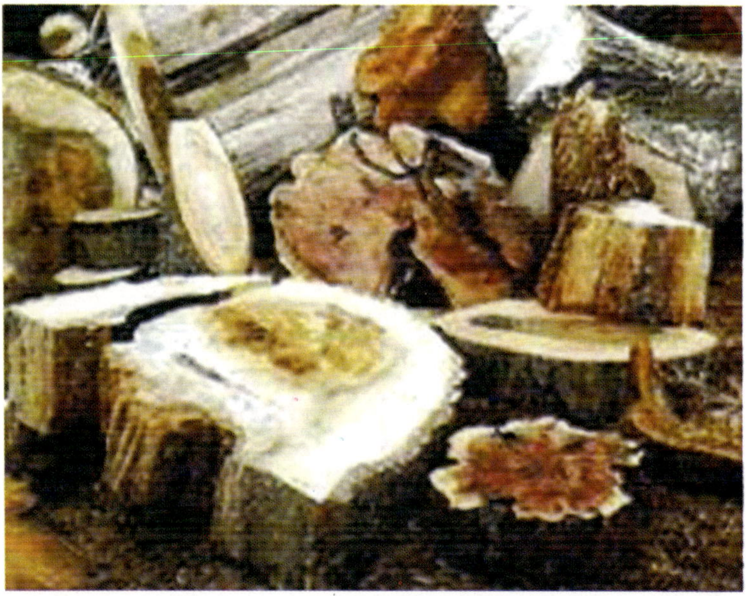

Pl. 12: Wooden logs, clearing of forests

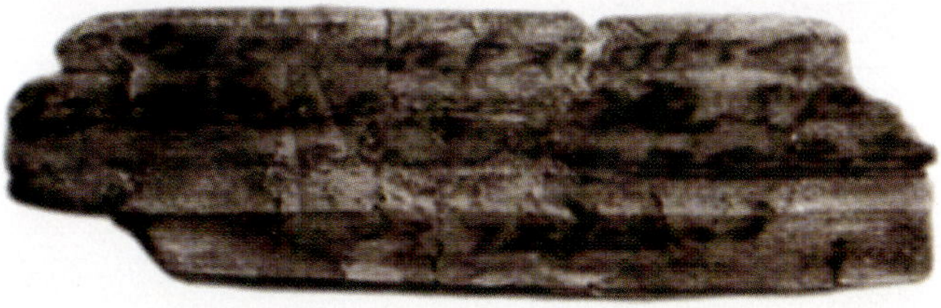

Pl. 13: Ancient Kharosti writings on wood from Central Asia

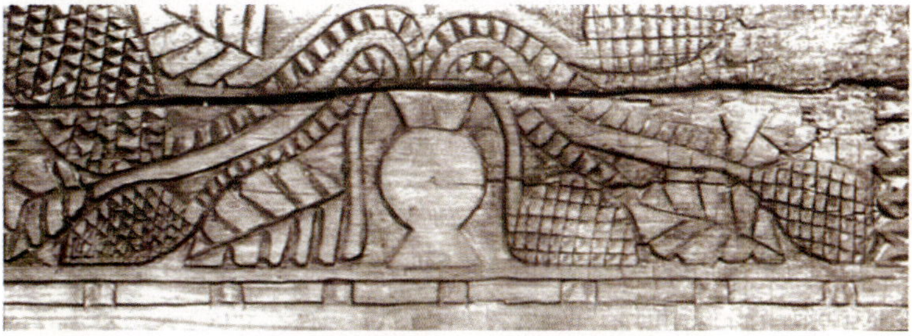

Pl. 14: Wooden architectural part of a Central Asian object — 3rd century CE

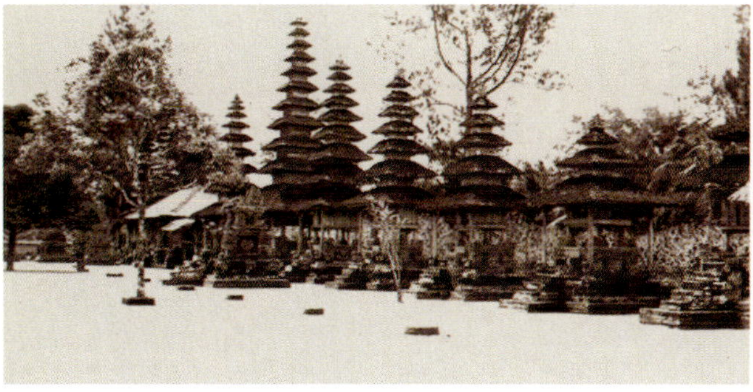

Pl. 15: Hindu wooden temple complex in Bali

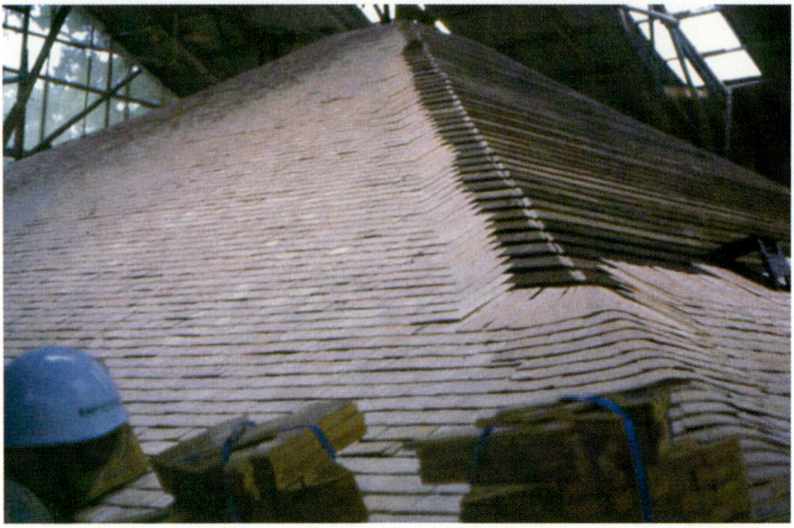

Pl. 16: Wooden structures in Japan being reconstructed

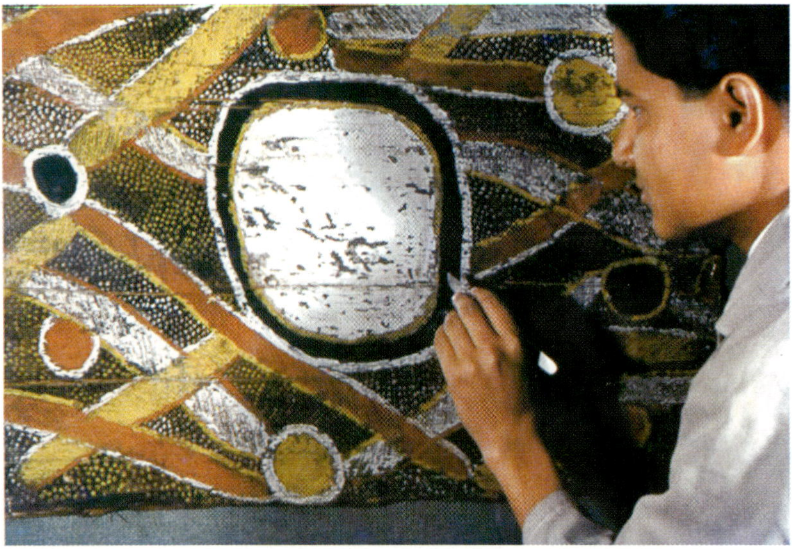

Pl. 17: Aborigine painting on bark from Australia

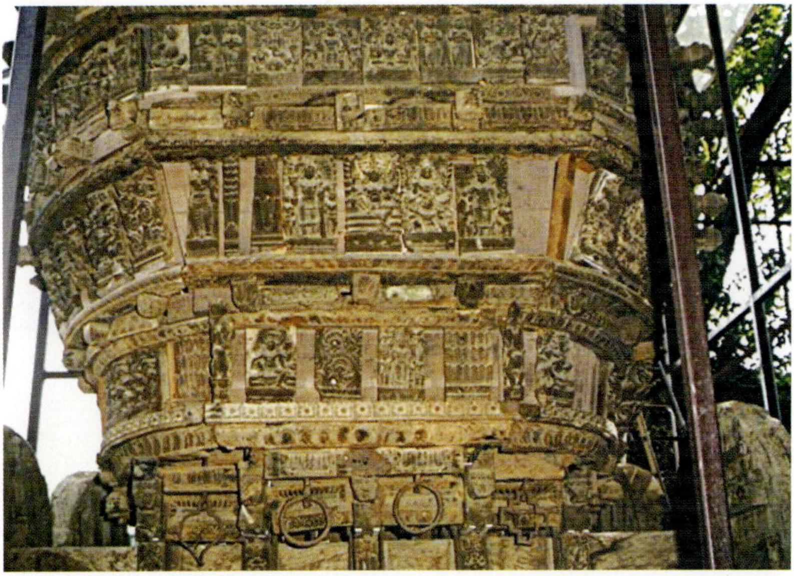

Pl. 18: Wooden Ratha from south India

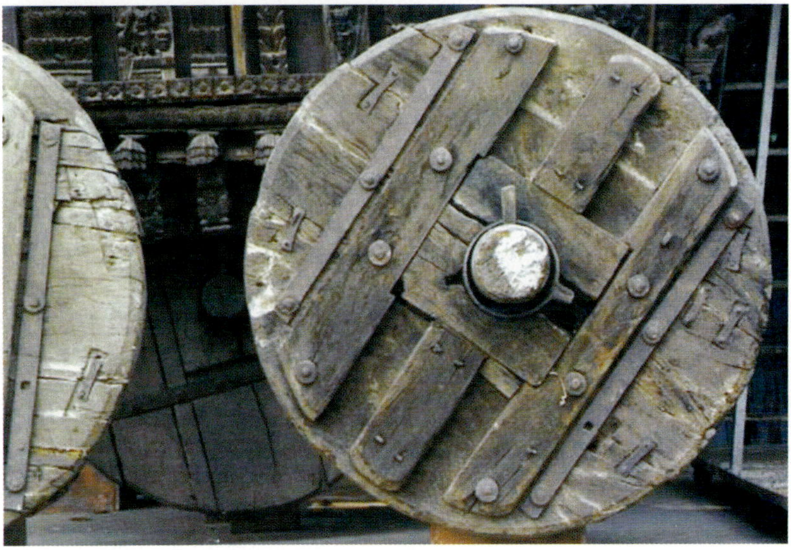

Pl. 19: Ratha on wheels to take village deity in a procession

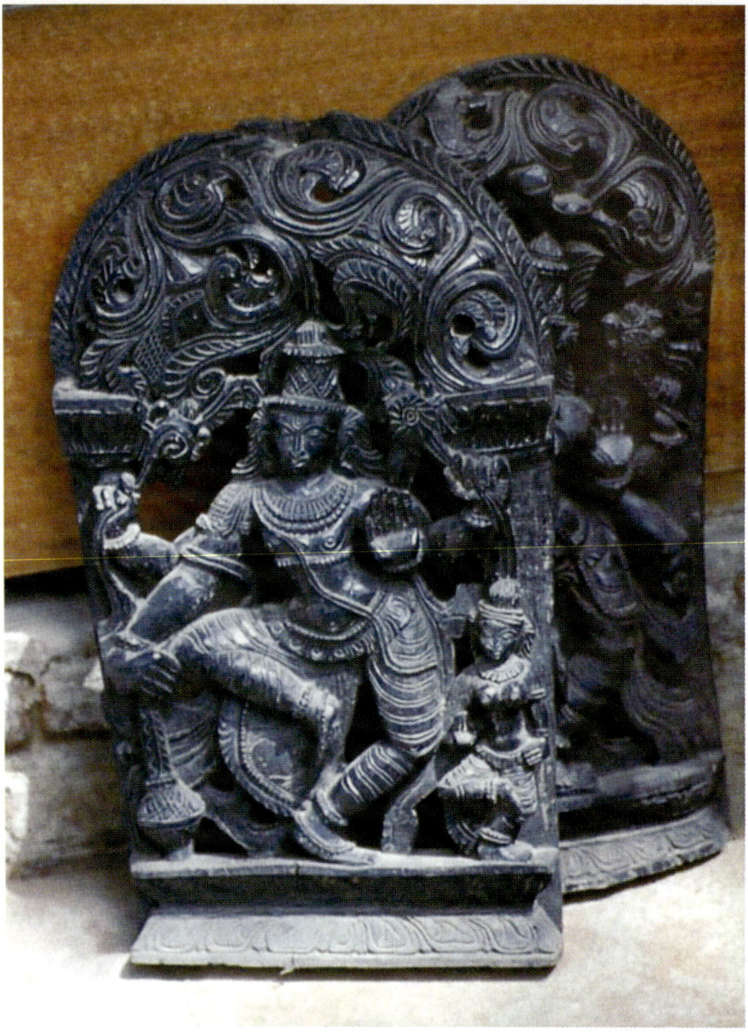

Pl. 20: Modern wood-worker carving a fake

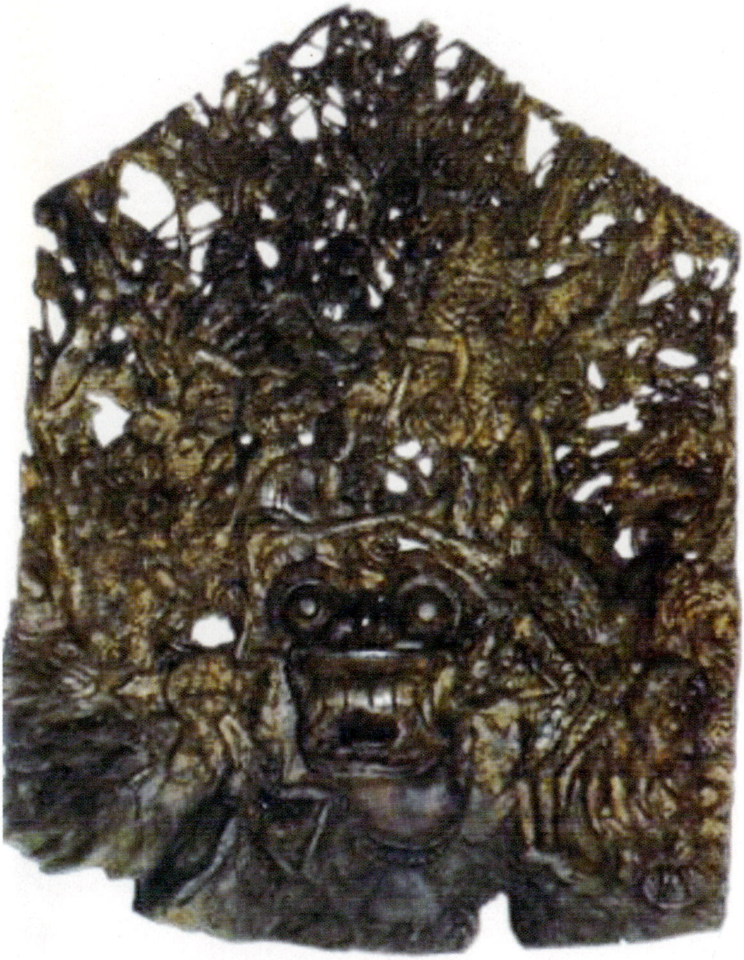

Pl. 21: Indonesian wood-carving as a craft

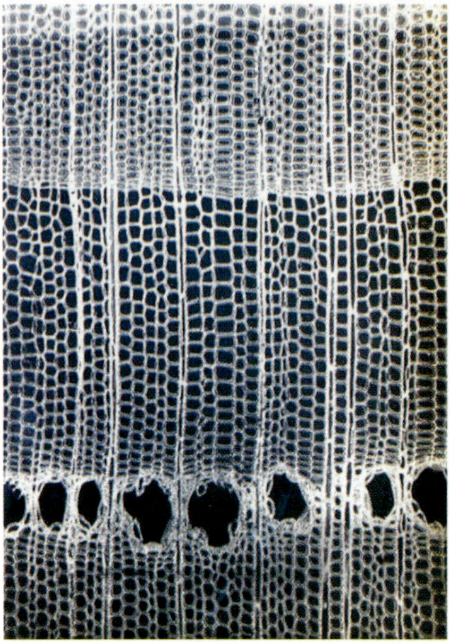

Pl. 22: Gymnosperm (softwood) cross section showing resin canal

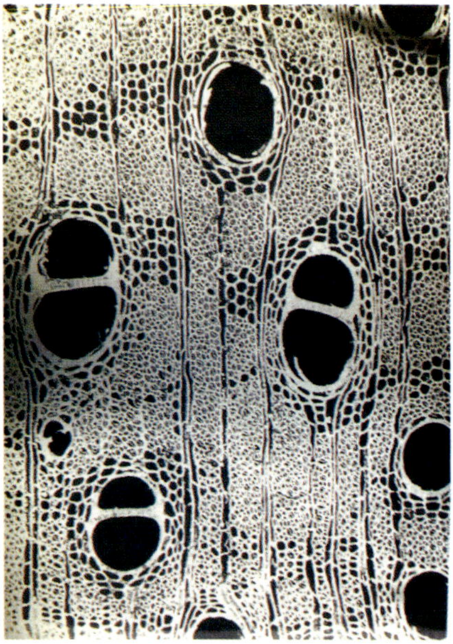

Pl. 23: Angiosperm (hardwood) cross section showing porous structure

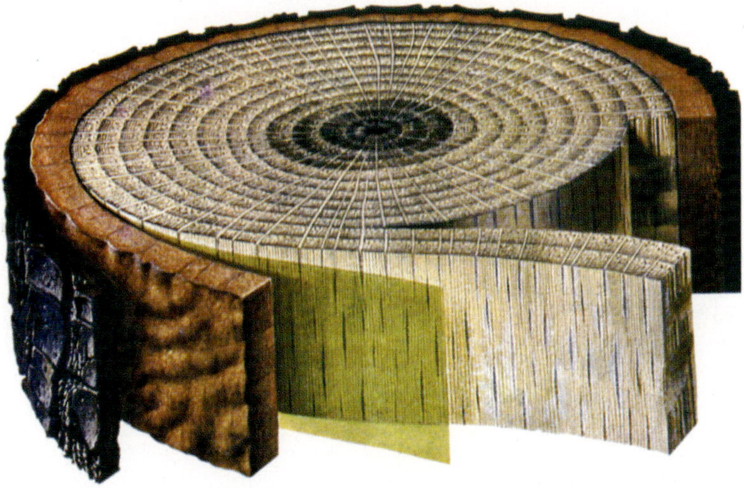

Pl. 24: Cross section of a log showing various details

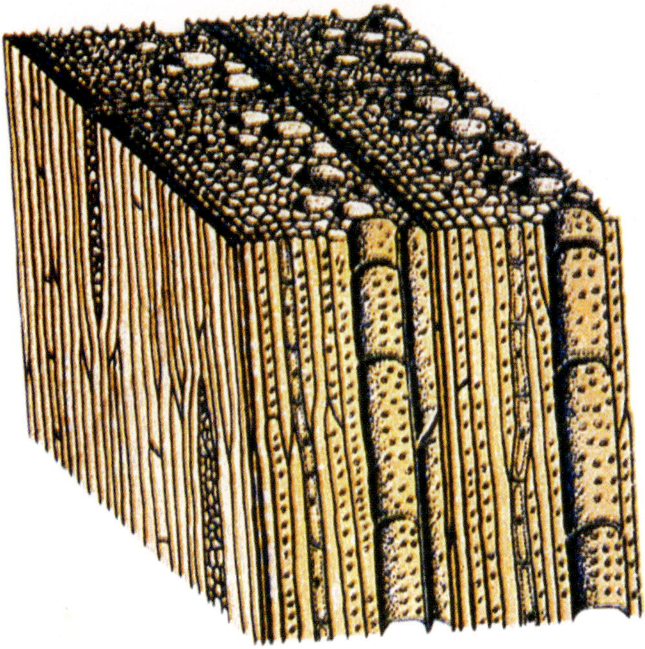

Pl. 25: Xylem (heart wood) on three planes

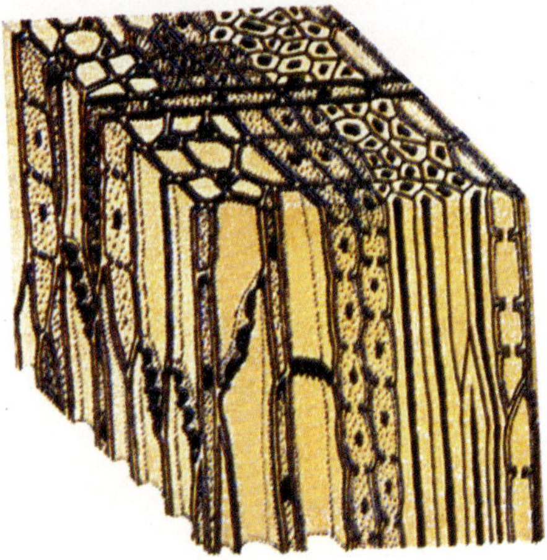

Pl. 26: Phloem (sap wood) on three planes

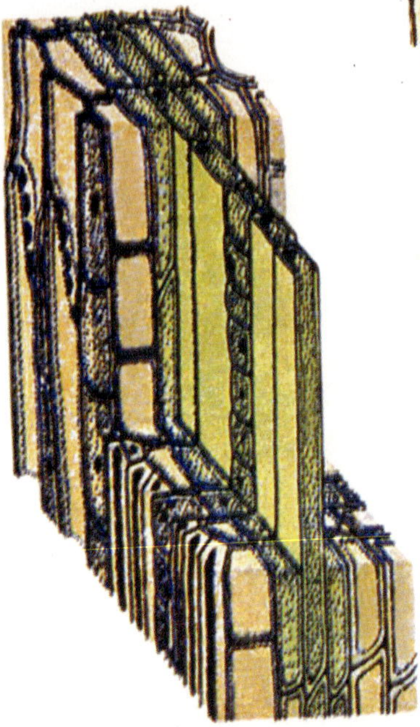

Pl. 27: Cambium on three planes

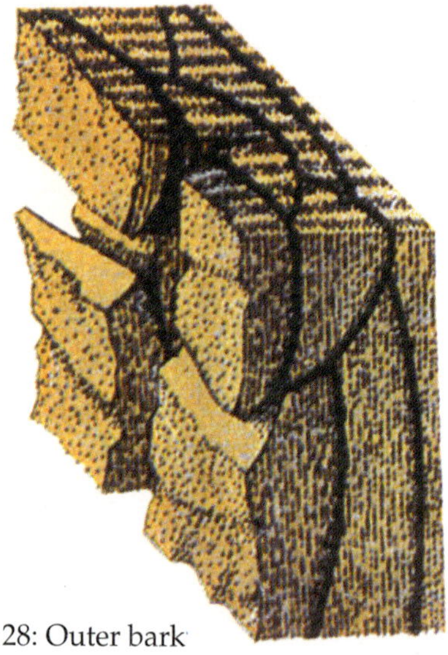

Pl. 28: Outer bark

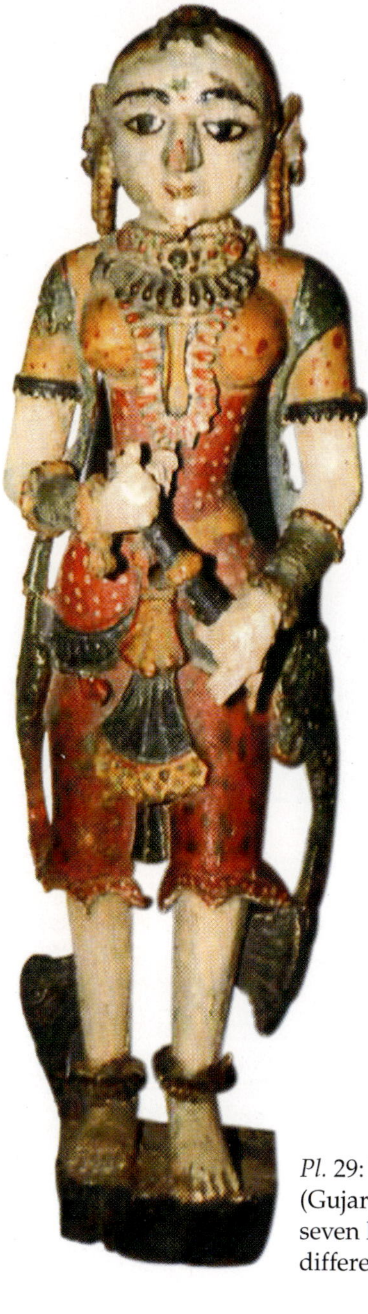

Pl. 29: Wooden statue (Gujarat) having seven layers of paint at different times

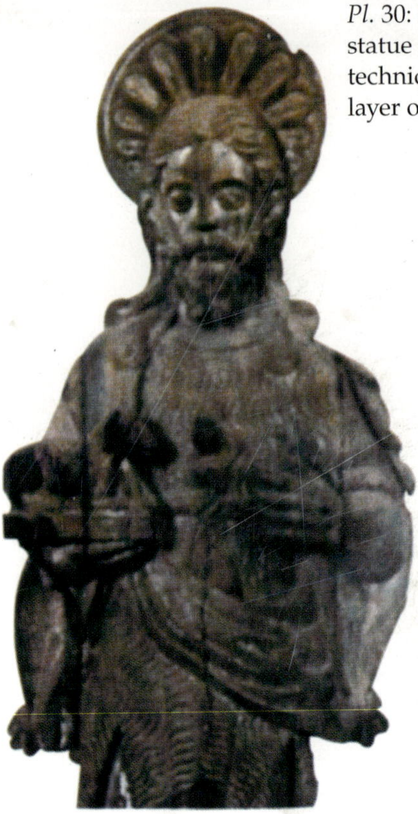

Pl. 30: Painted wooden statue (Goa) having faulty technique — very thin layer of gesso

Pl. 31: Painted panel (Goa) having thick deposits of dust

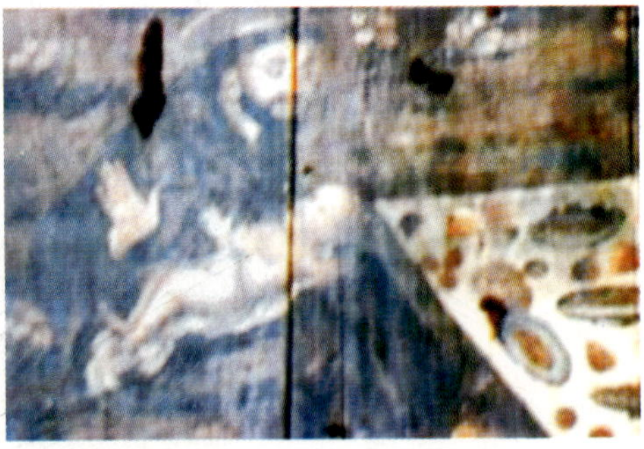

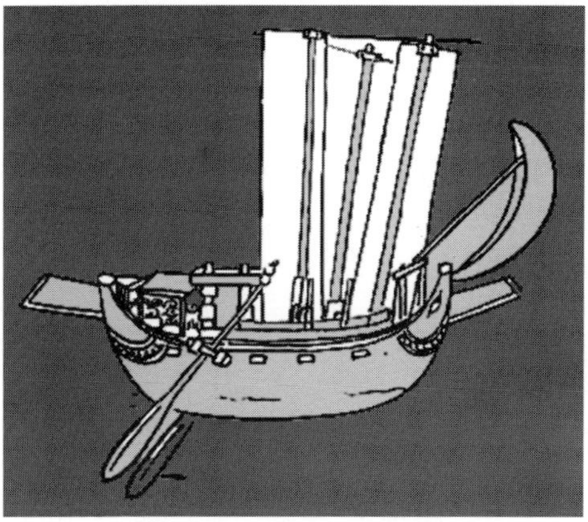

fig. 1: Representation of a wooden ship in the Ajanta murals

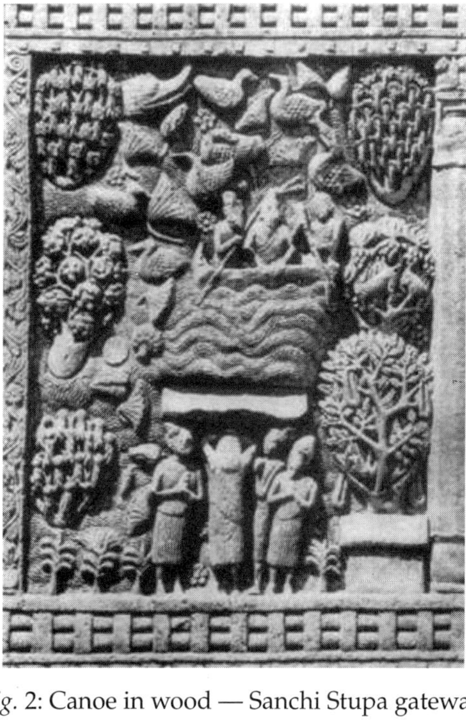

fig. 2: Canoe in wood — Sanchi Stupa gateway

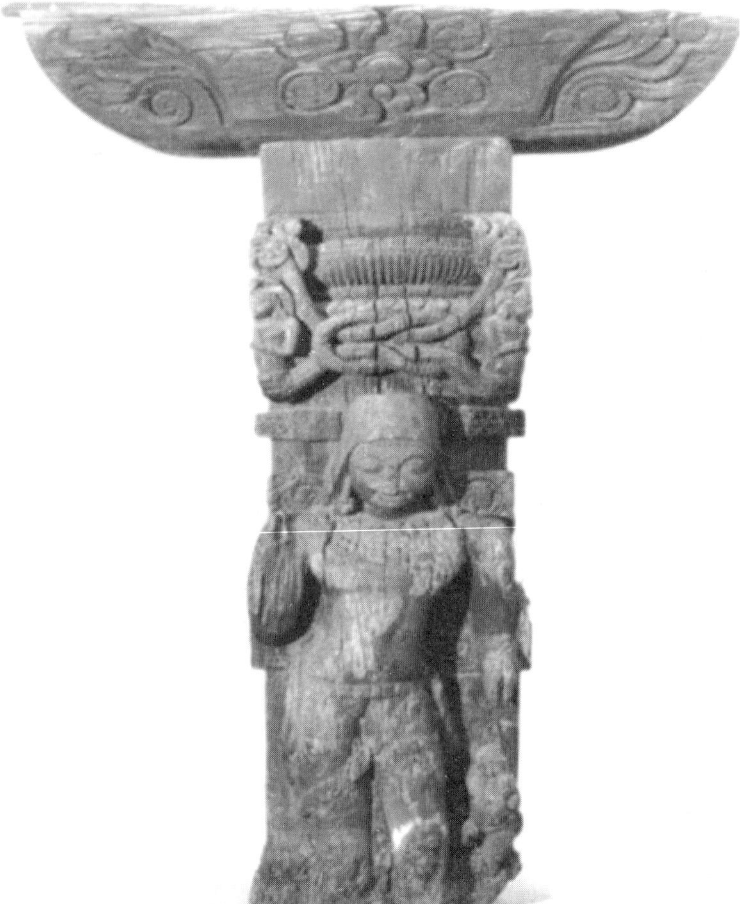

fig. 3: Vishnu image from
Katarmal Almora
made of deodar

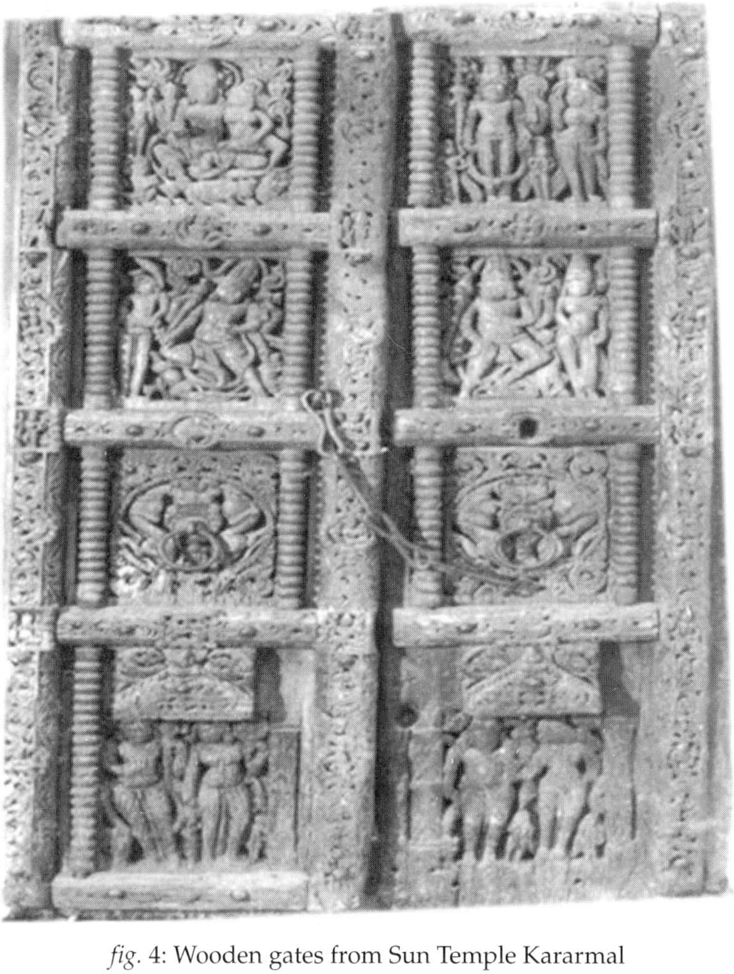

fig. 4: Wooden gates from Sun Temple Kararmal Almora made of shisham

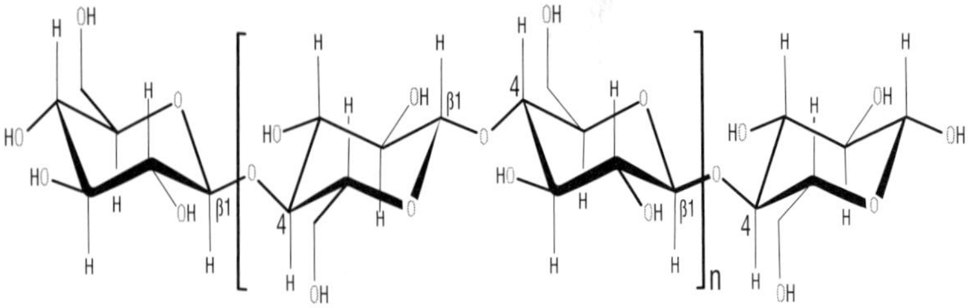

fig. 5: Cellulose polymer long chain

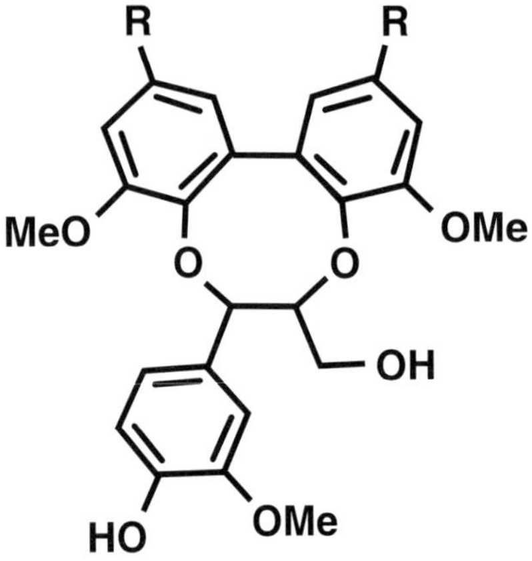

1

fig. 6: Monomer unit of lignin

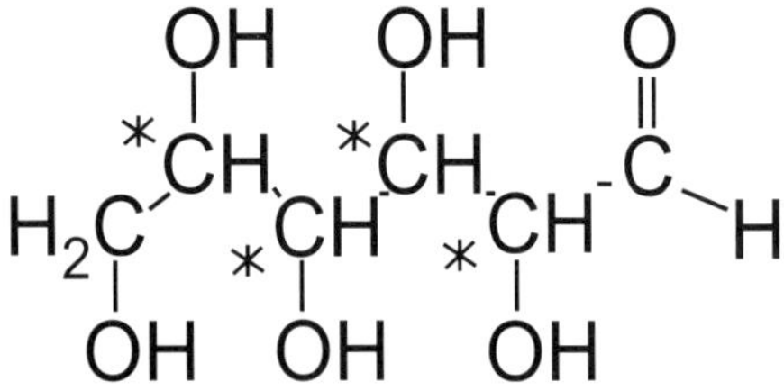

∗ Chiral Carbons

fig. 7: Glucose unit

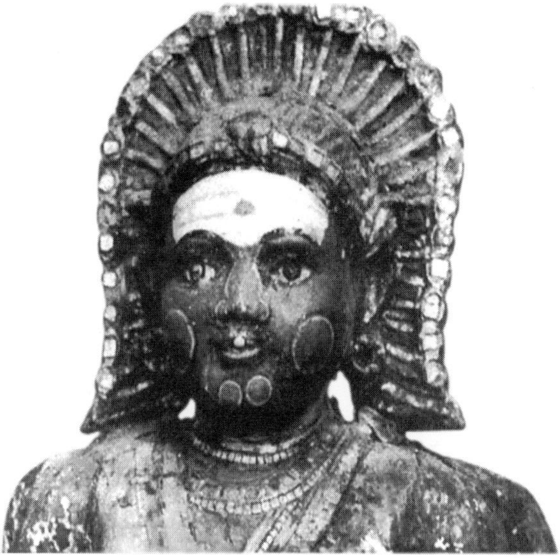

fig. 8: Painted wooden object carved in parts

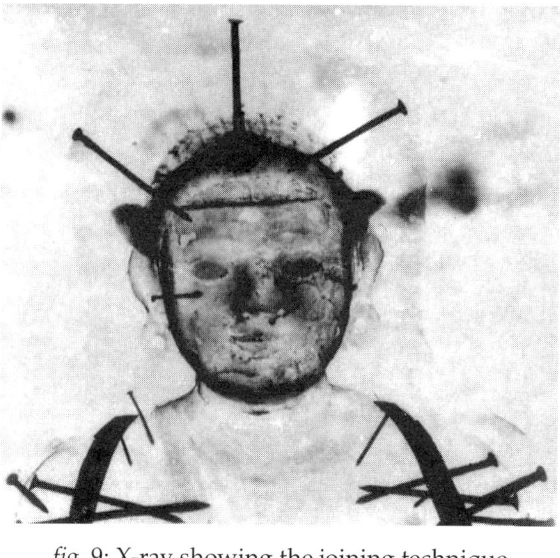

fig. 9: X-ray showing the joining technique using iron nails

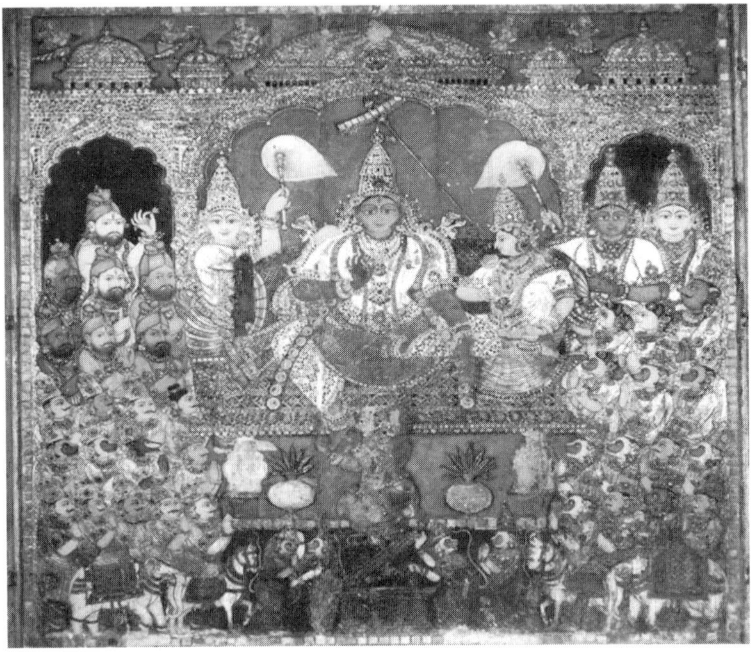

fig. 10: Ram Durbar-Tanjore painting showing damage of various natures

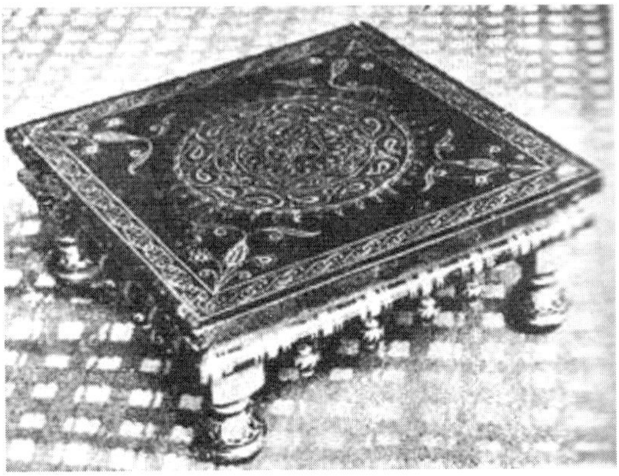

fig. 11: Coloured Lac turnery work on a small wooden table from Sankheda

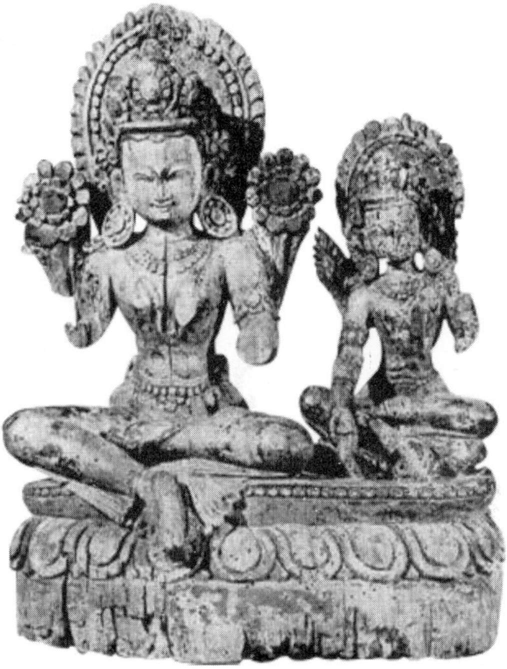

fig. 12: Wooden statue showing crack and decay of the lower part

fig. 13: Lower part of a wooden statue showing wide crack

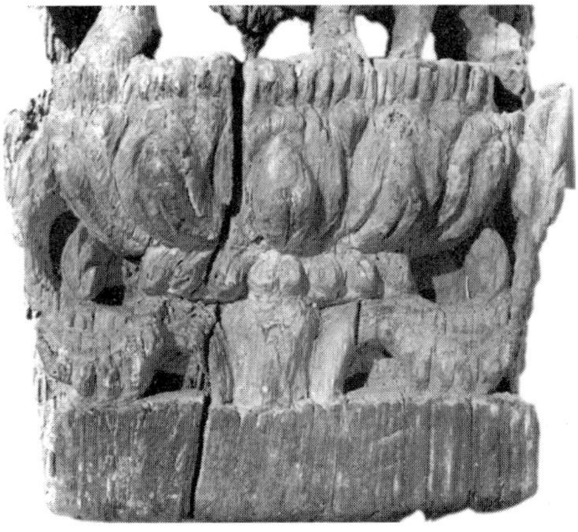

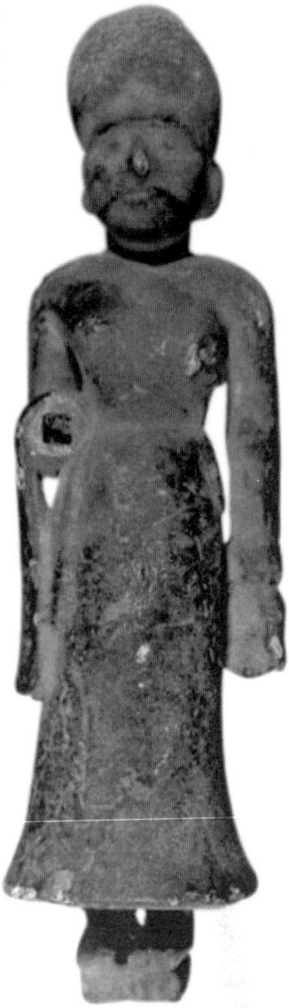

fig. 14: Painted wooden statue (Gujarat) having darkened varnish layer

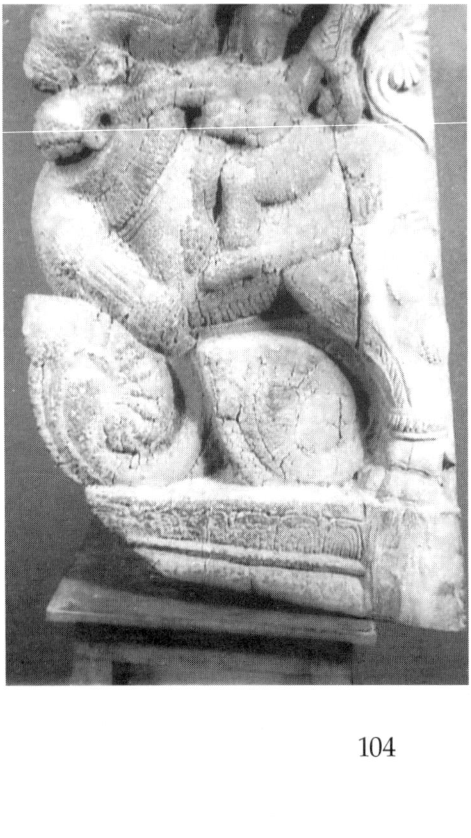

fig. 15: Temple bracket from Kerala having deposits of various compositions hiding the details

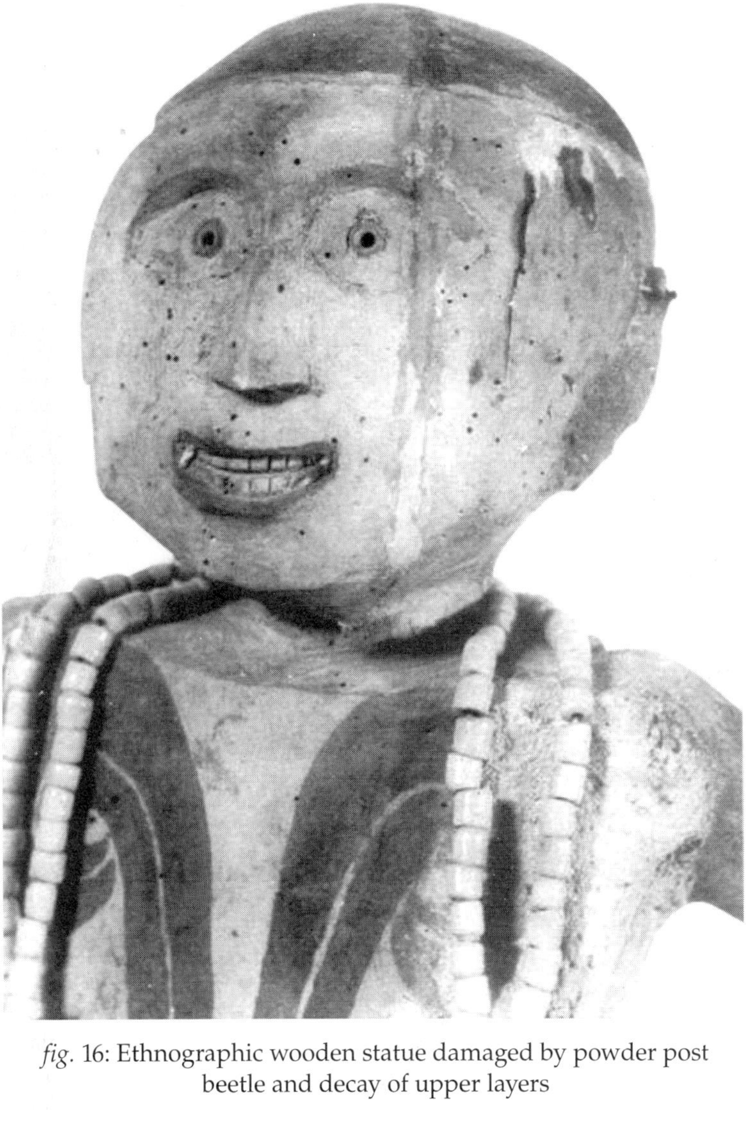

fig. 16: Ethnographic wooden statue damaged by powder post beetle and decay of upper layers

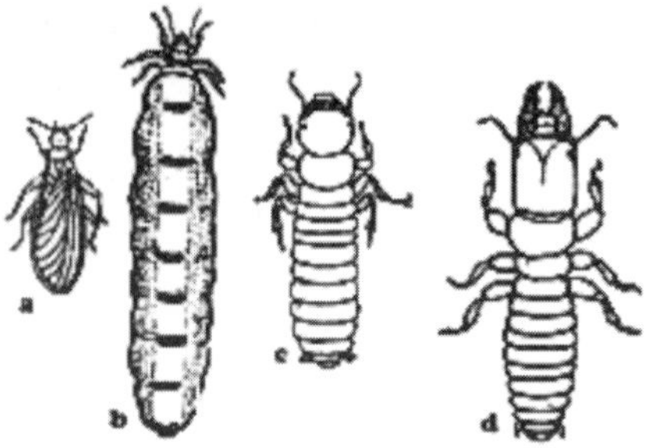

fig. 17: Termite Family (a) King; (b) Queen; (c) Worker; and (d) Soldier

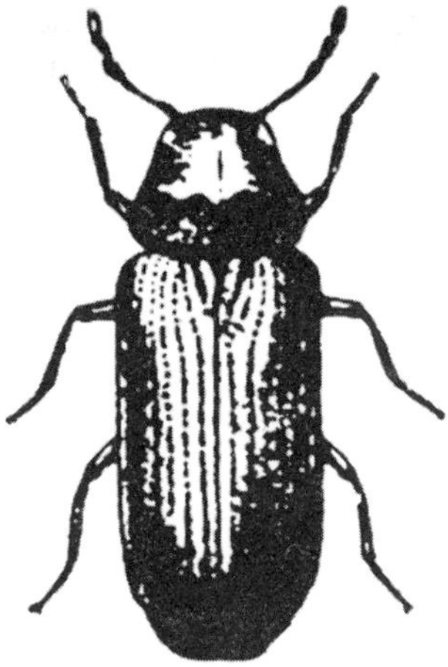

fig. 18: Furniture Beetle

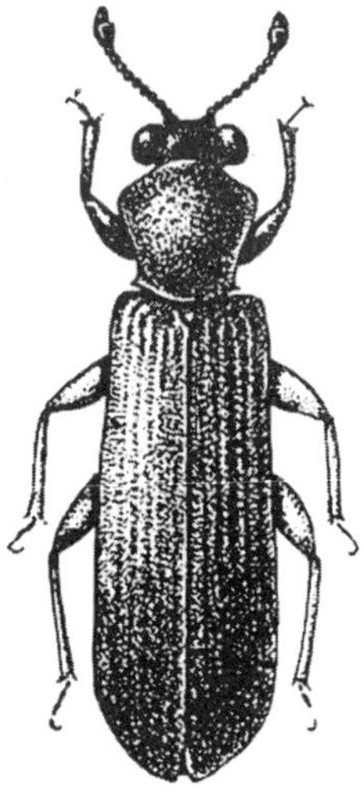

fig. 19: Death Watch Beetle

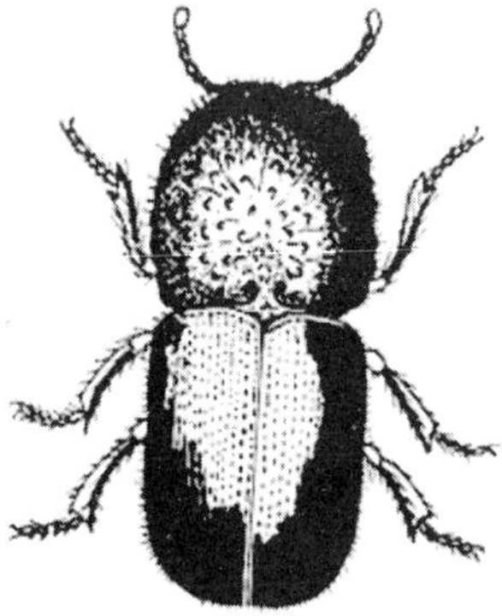

fig. 20: Bamboo Powder post Beetle

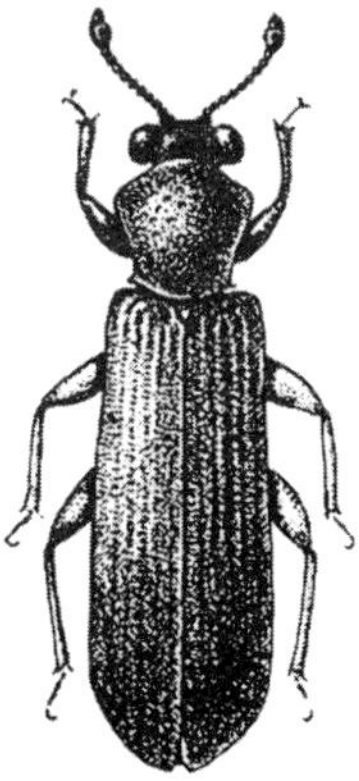

fig. 21: Powder post Beetle

fig. 22: Wooden statue heavily damage by termites

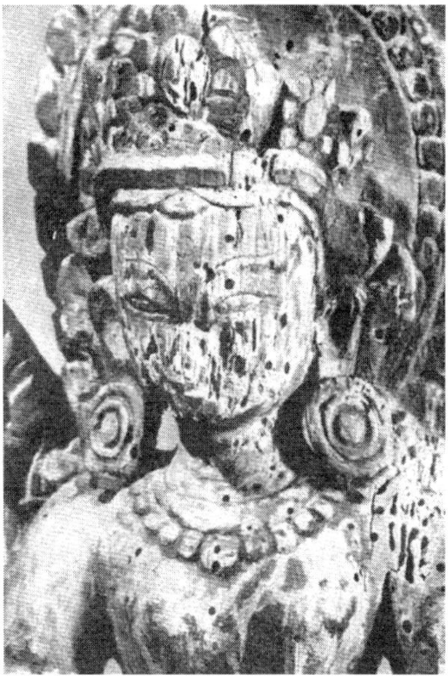

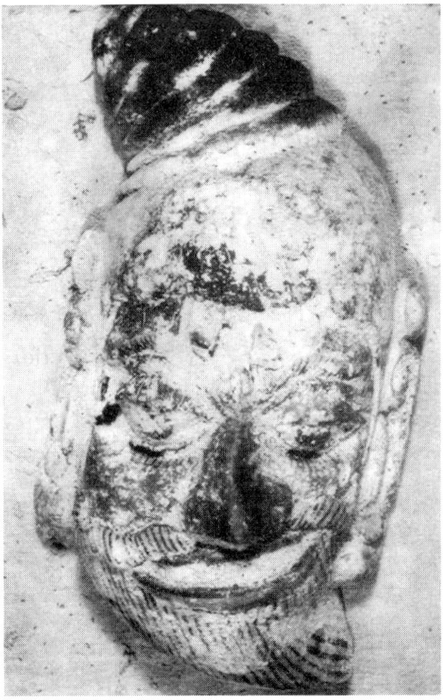

fig. 23: Wooden head badly affected by powder post beetle covering the surface details

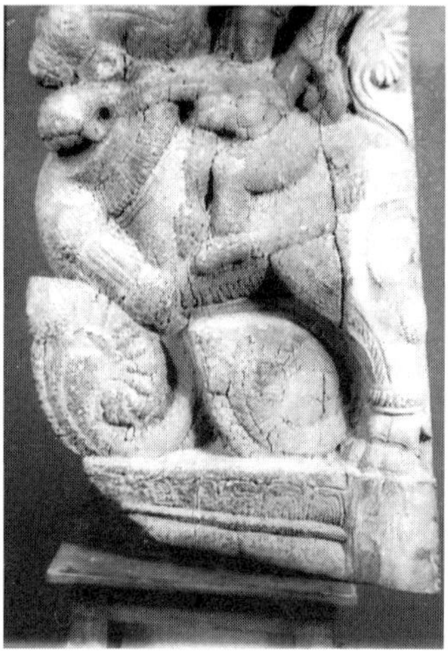

fig. 24: Temple bracket from Kerala before treatment hiding the details

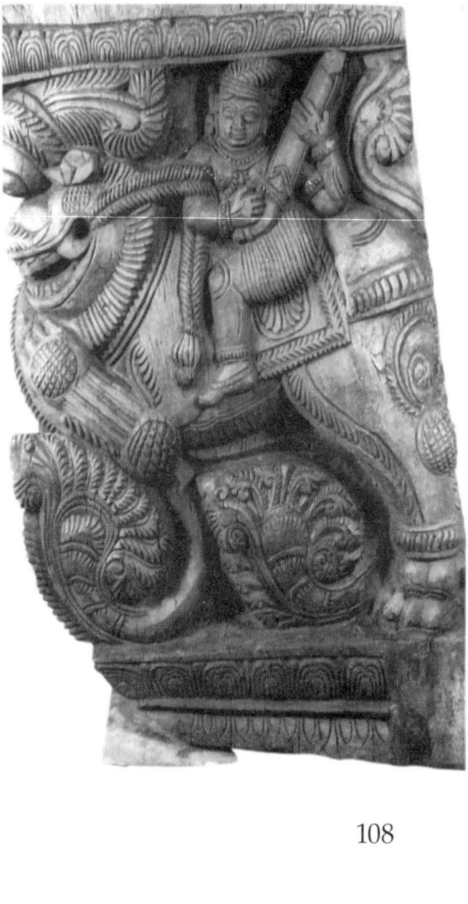

fig. 25: Temple bracket from Kerala after treatment making all details clear

fig. 26: Painted wooden statue before and after treatment

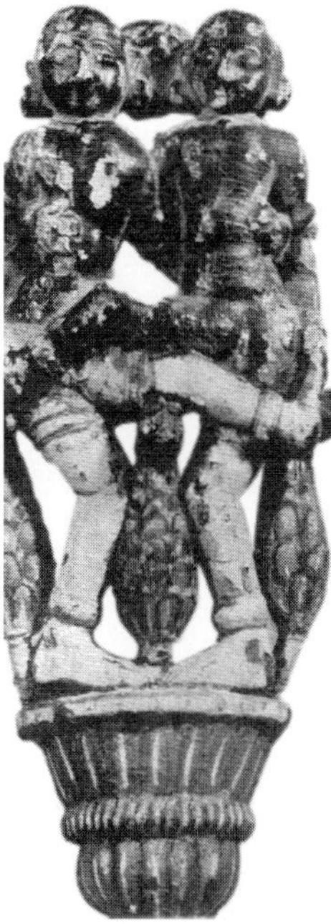

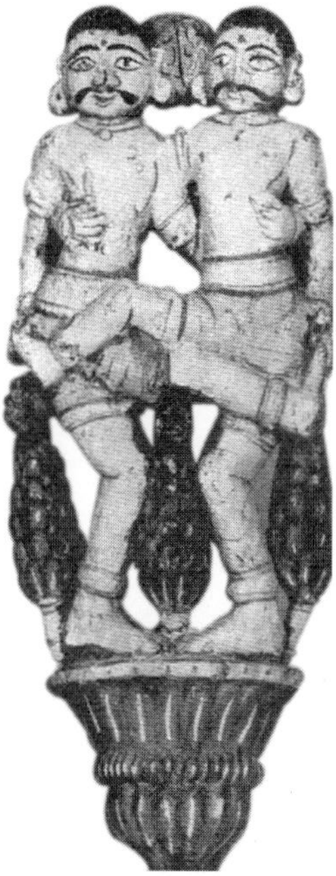

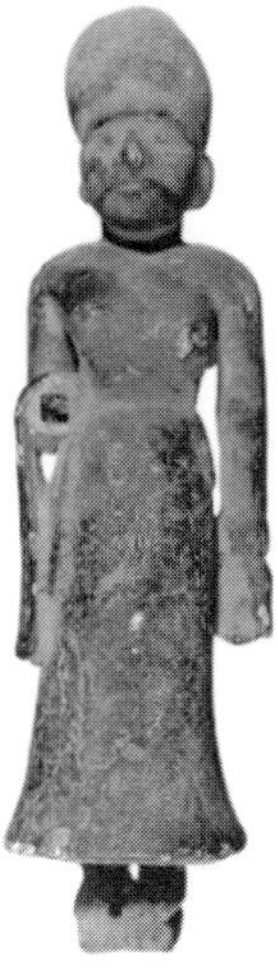

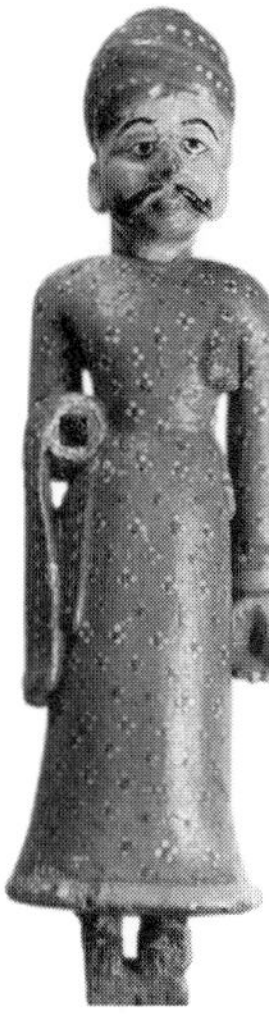

fig. 27: Painted wooden image before and after removal of darkened varnish

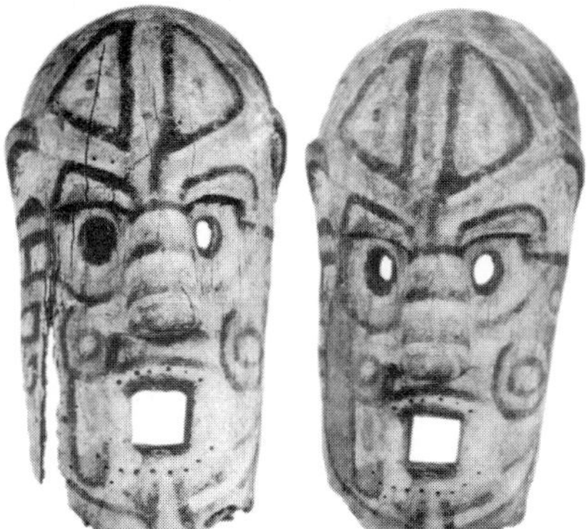

fig. 28: Wooden mask before and after conservation

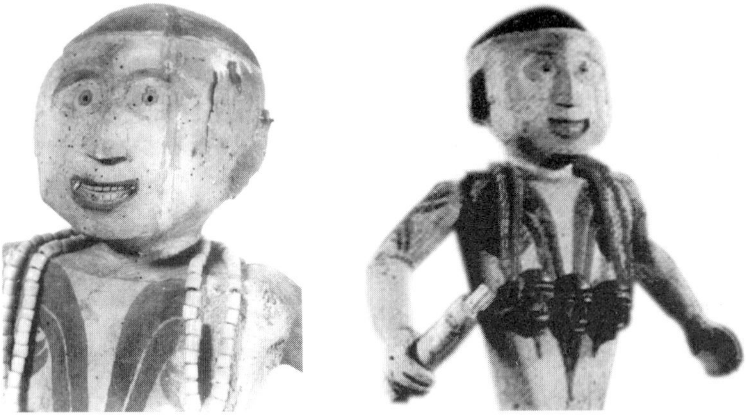

fig. 29: Ethnographic statue before and after restoration

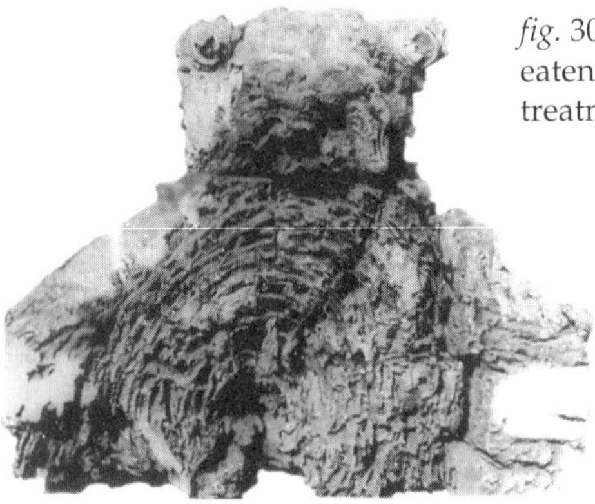

fig. 30: End of the doorway eaten by termites before treatment

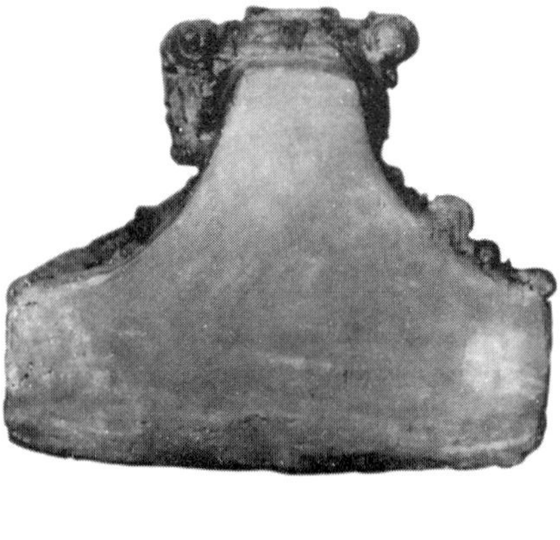

fig. 31: End of doorway after disinfections and consolidation with wax and resin solution

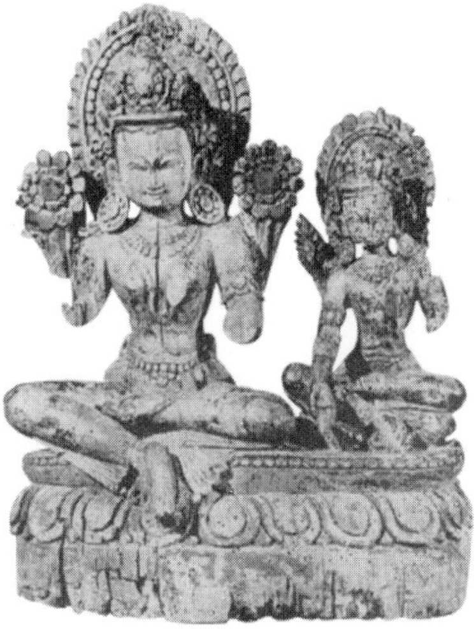

fig. 32: Wooden image from Nepal before treatment

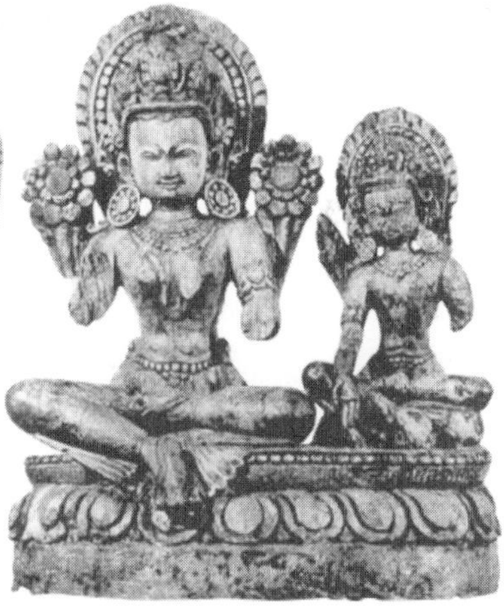

fig. 33: Wooden image from Nepal after treatment and restoration

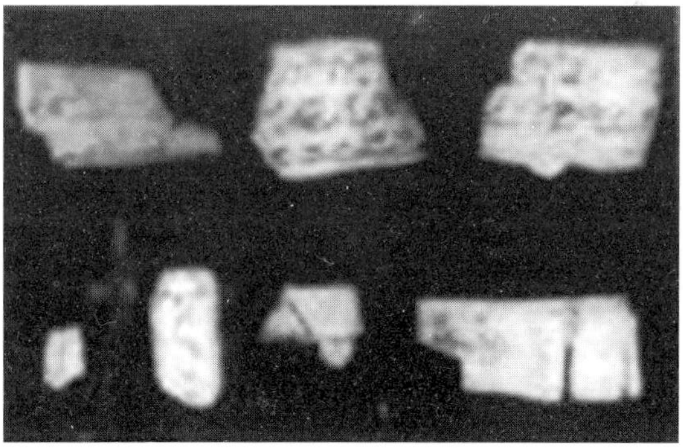

fig. 34: Wooden tablets from Central Asia broken into many pieces before treatment

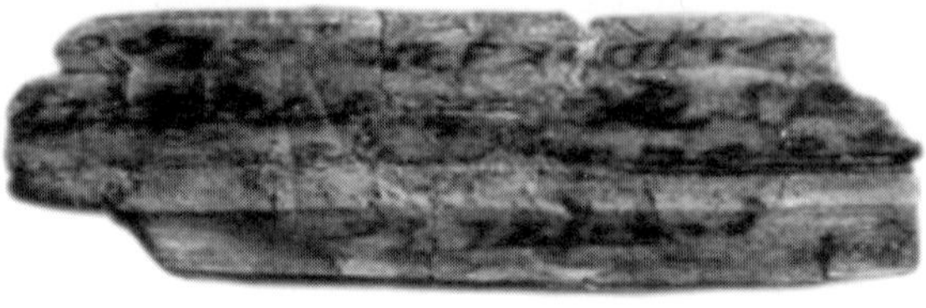

fig. 35: Wooden tablets from Central Asia after treatment, joining and restoration

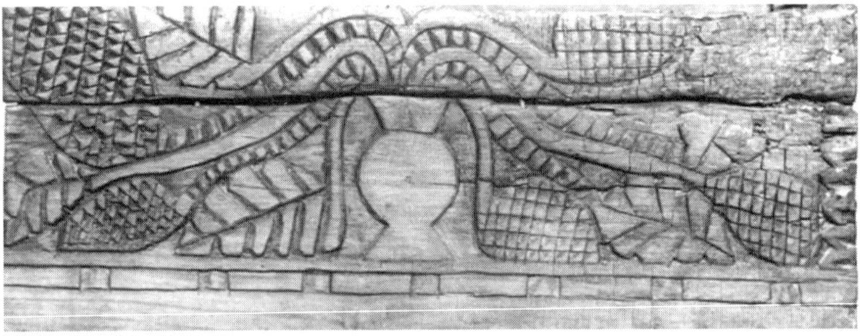

fig. 36: Wooden object from Central Asia 3rd century CE with Purnaghata before treatment

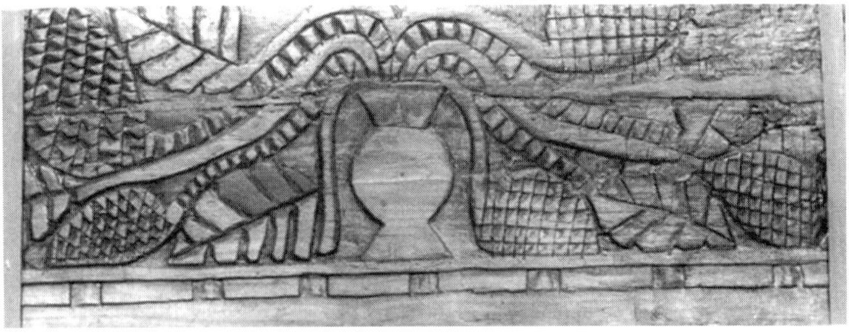

fig. 37: Wooden object from Central Asia after conservation and restoration

Index